CLASSIC INDIAN STORIES • PRATILIPI COMICS INDIA •

RABINDRANATH

TAGORE

KABULIWALA
THE POSTMASTER

First published by Westland Books, a division of Nasadiya Technologies Private Limited, in 2024

No. 269/2B, First Floor, 'Irai Arul', Vimalraj Street, Nethaji Nagar, Alapakkam Main Road, Maduravoyal, Chennai 600095

Westland and the Westland logo are the trademarks of Nasadiya Technologies Private Limited, or its affiliates.

Copyright © Nasadiya Technologies Private Limited, 2024

This comic is an adaptation of two short stories —*Kabuliwala* and *The Postmaster*.

ISBN: 9789360450083

10 9 8 7 6 5 4 3 2 1

This is a work of fiction. Names, characters, organisations, places, events and incidents are either products of the author's imagination or used fictitiously.

All rights reserved

Book design by New Media Line Creations, New Delhi

Printed at Parksons Graphics Pvt. Ltd.

No part of this book may be reproduced, or stored in a retrieval system, or transmitted in any form or by any means, electronic, mechanical, photocopying, recording, or otherwise, without express written permission of the publisher.

KABULIWALA

MY FIVE-YEAR-OLD DAUGHTER MINI TALKED NON-STOP.
HER MOTHER OFTEN TOLD HER TO TALK LESS. BUT NOT ME.
TO ME, IT DIDN'T FEEL NORMAL WHEN MINI WAS QUIET. SO, WE OFTEN SPENT TIME TALKING TO EACH OTHER.
ONE MORNING, MINI WALKED INTO MY ROOM ...
Baba, Ram Dayal calls a kak, 'kauwa'. He doesn't know anything.
Yes, Mini?

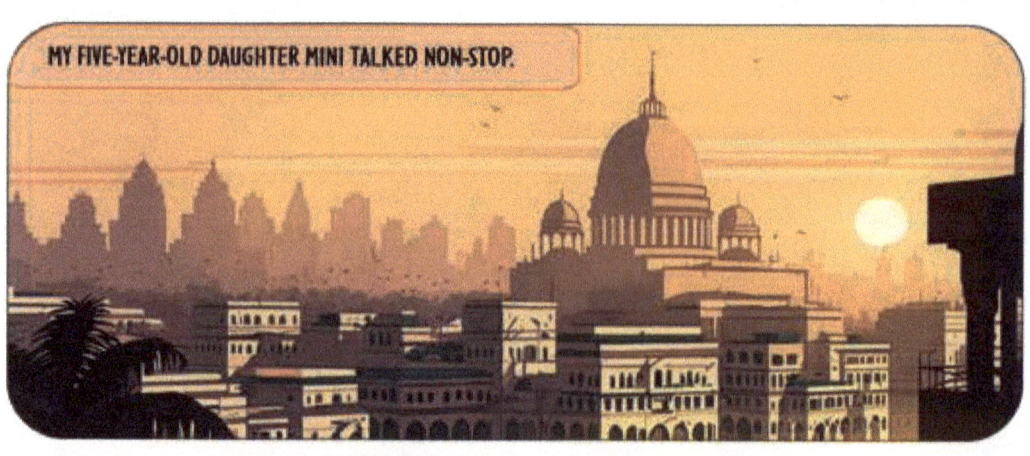

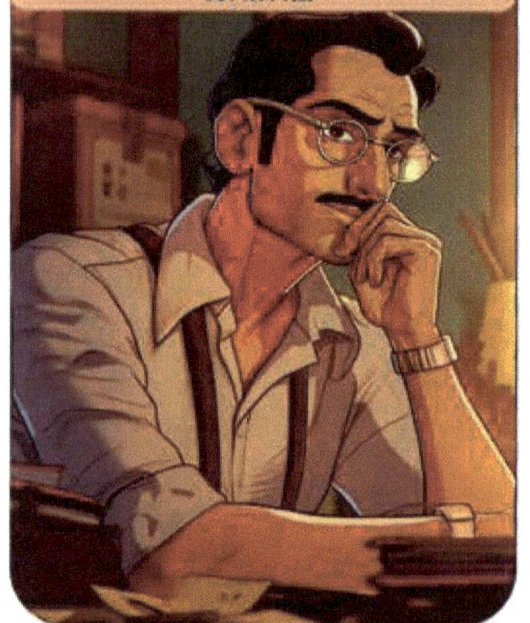

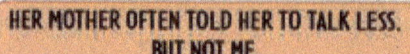

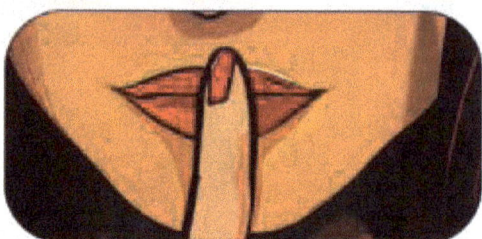

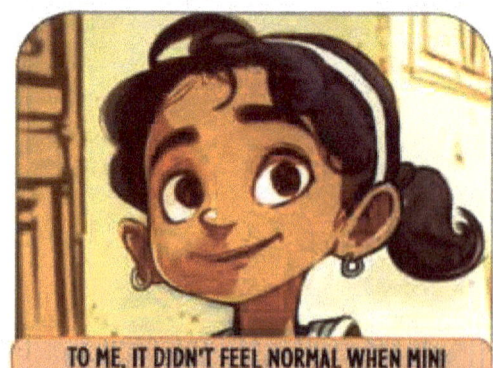

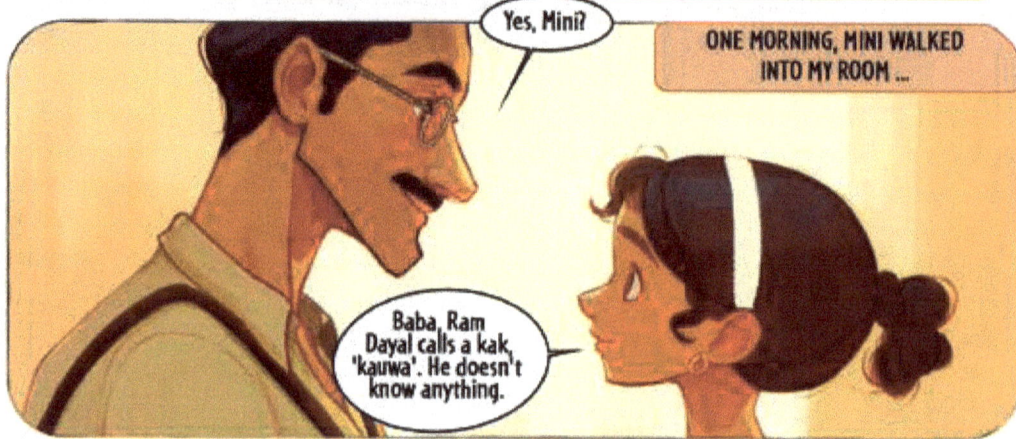

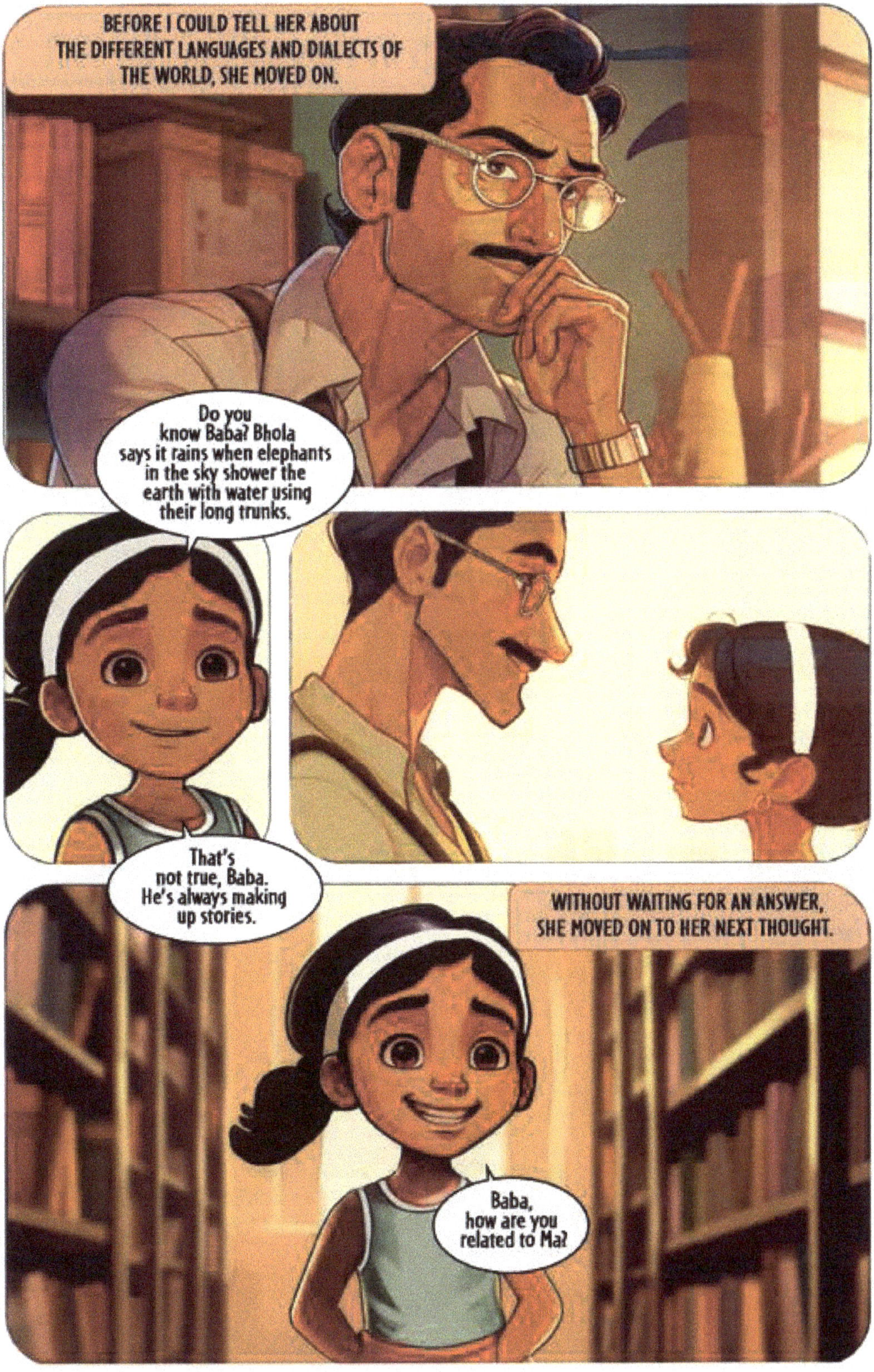
BEFORE I COULD TELL HER ABOUT THE DIFFERENT LANGUAGES AND DIALECTS OF THE WORLD, SHE MOVED ON.
Do you know Baba? Bhola says it rains when elephants in the sky shower the earth with water using their long trunks.
That's not true, Baba. He's always making up stories.
WITHOUT WAITING FOR AN ANSWER, SHE MOVED ON TO HER NEXT THOUGHT.
Baba, how are you related to Ma?

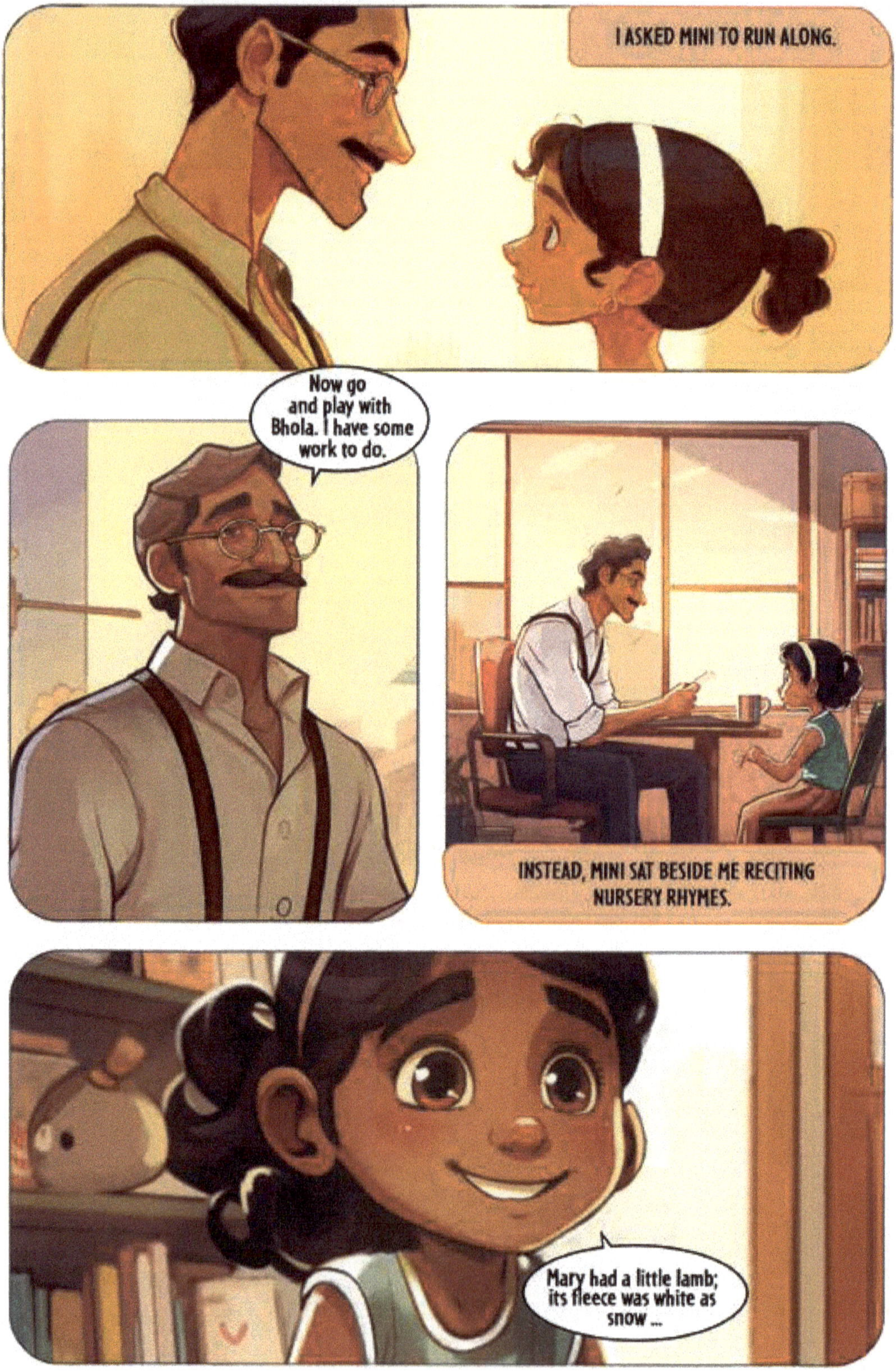
I ASKED MINI TO RUN ALONG.
Now go and play with Bhola. I have some work to do.
INSTEAD, MINI SAT BESIDE ME RECITING NURSERY RHYMES.
Mary had a little lamb; its fleece was white as snow ...

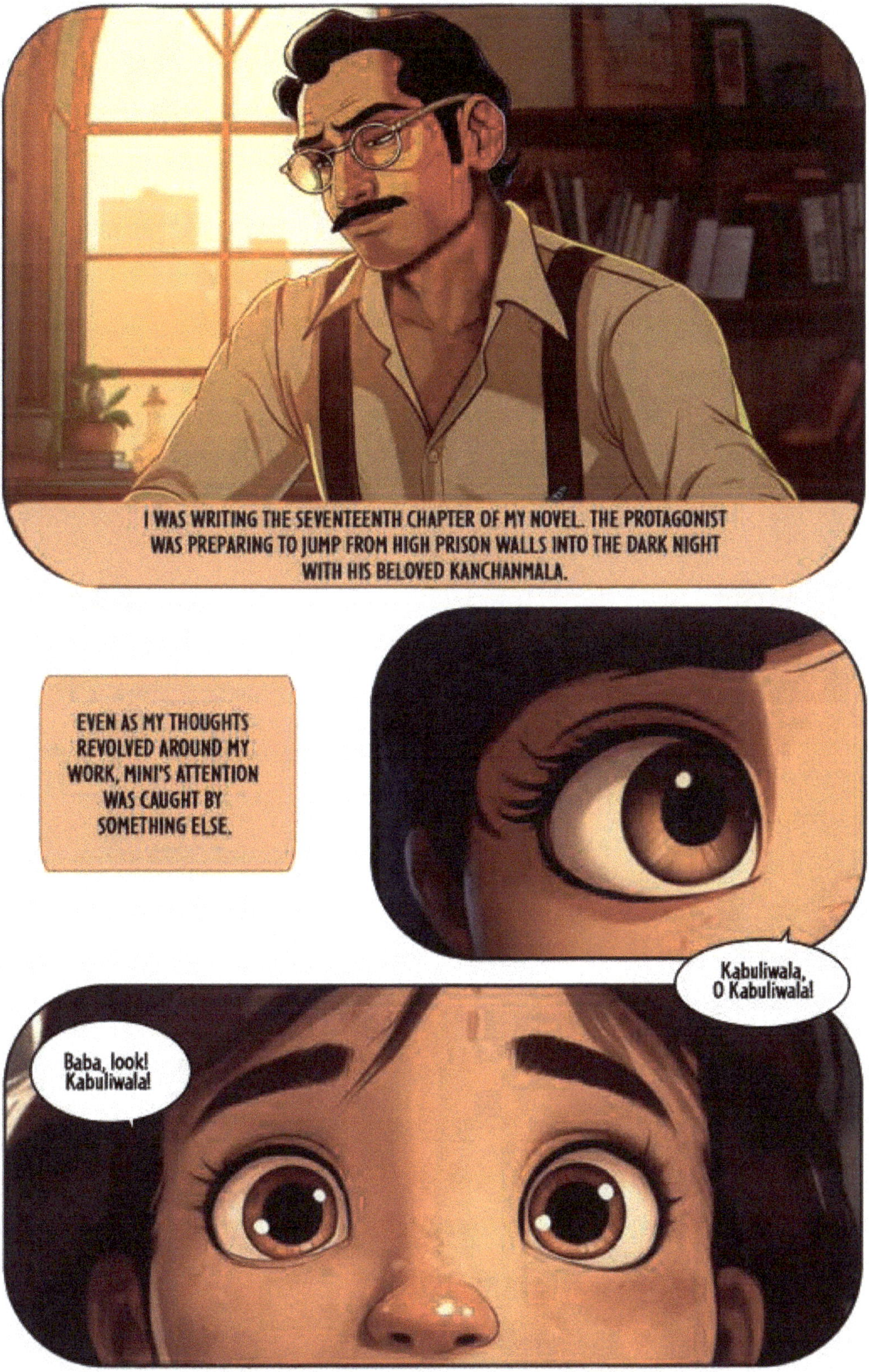
I WAS WRITING THE SEVENTEENTH CHAPTER OF MY NOVEL. THE PROTAGONIST WAS PREPARING TO JUMP FROM HIGH PRISON WALLS INTO THE DARK NIGHT WITH HIS BELOVED KANCHANMALA.
EVEN AS MY THOUGHTS REVOLVED AROUND MY WORK, MINI'S ATTENTION WAS CAUGHT BY SOMETHING ELSE.
Kabuliwala, O Kabuliwala!
Baba, look! Kabuliwala!

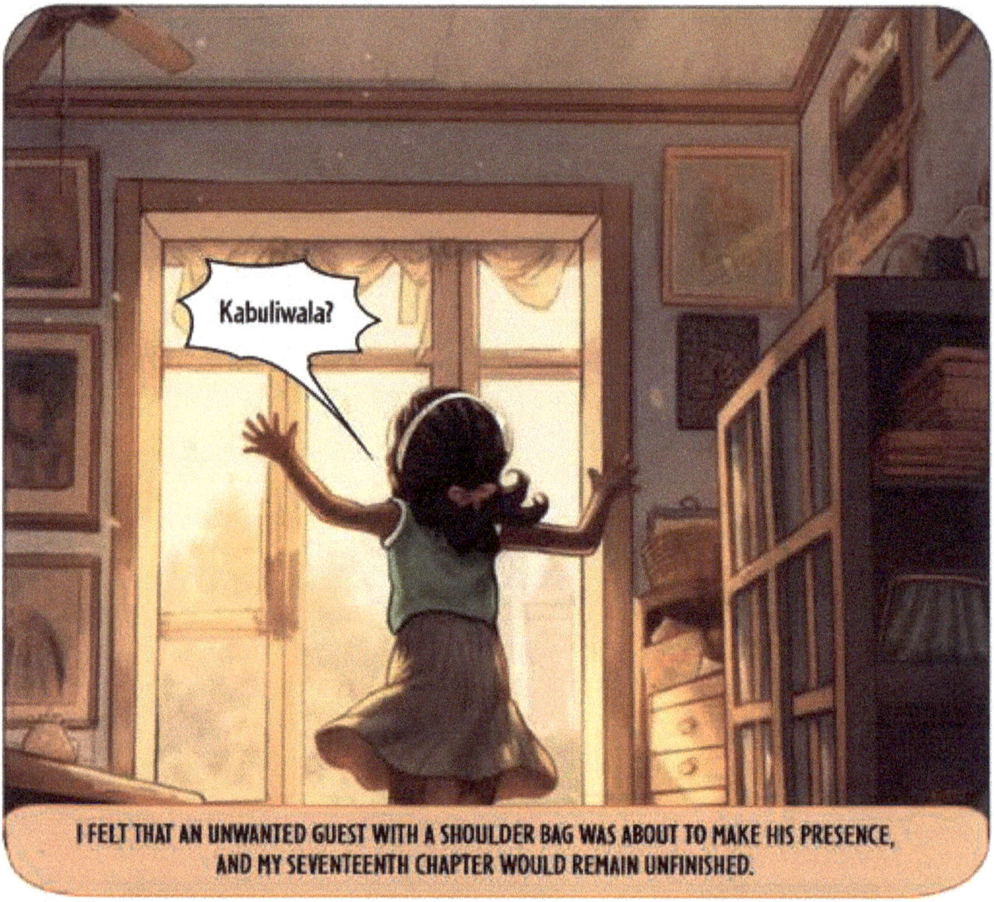
Kabuliwala?
I FELT THAT AN UNWANTED GUEST WITH A SHOULDER BAG WAS ABOUT TO MAKE HIS PRESENCE, AND MY SEVENTEENTH CHAPTER WOULD REMAIN UNFINISHED.

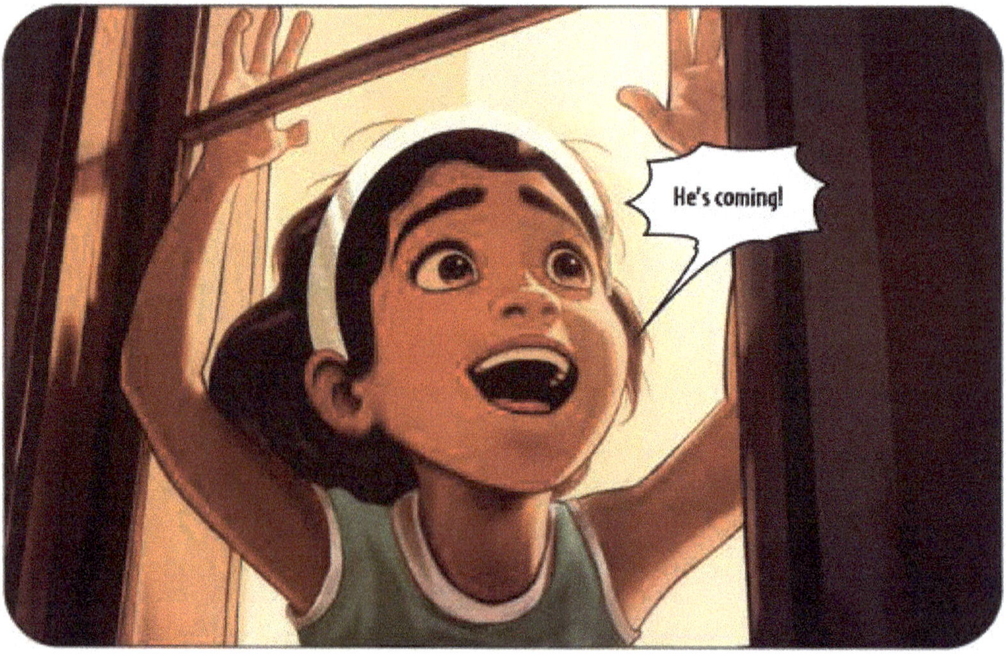
He's coming!

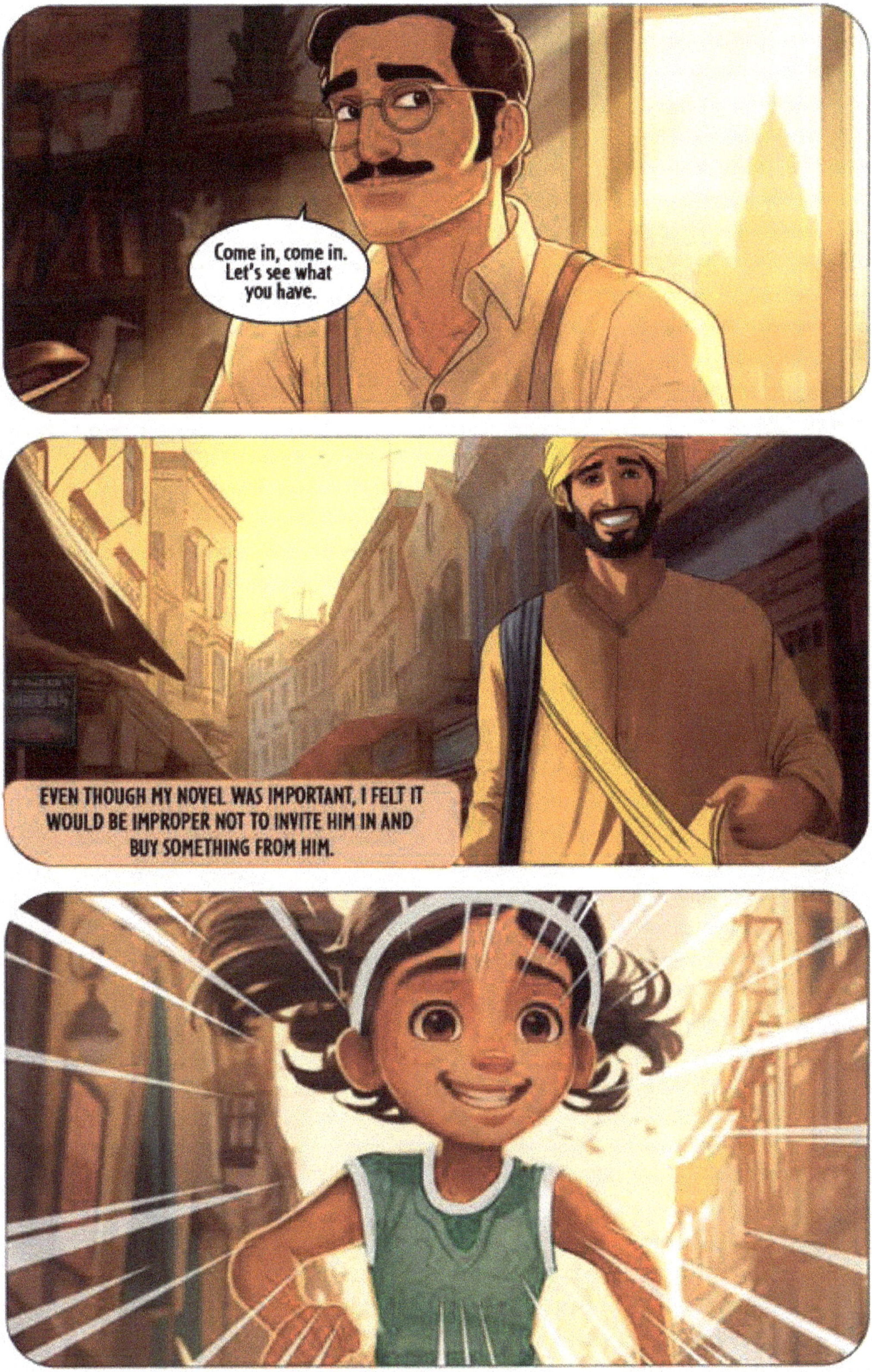
Come in, come in. Let's see what you have.
EVEN THOUGH MY NOVEL WAS IMPORTANT, I FELT IT WOULD BE IMPROPER NOT TO INVITE HIM IN AND BUY SOMETHING FROM HIM.

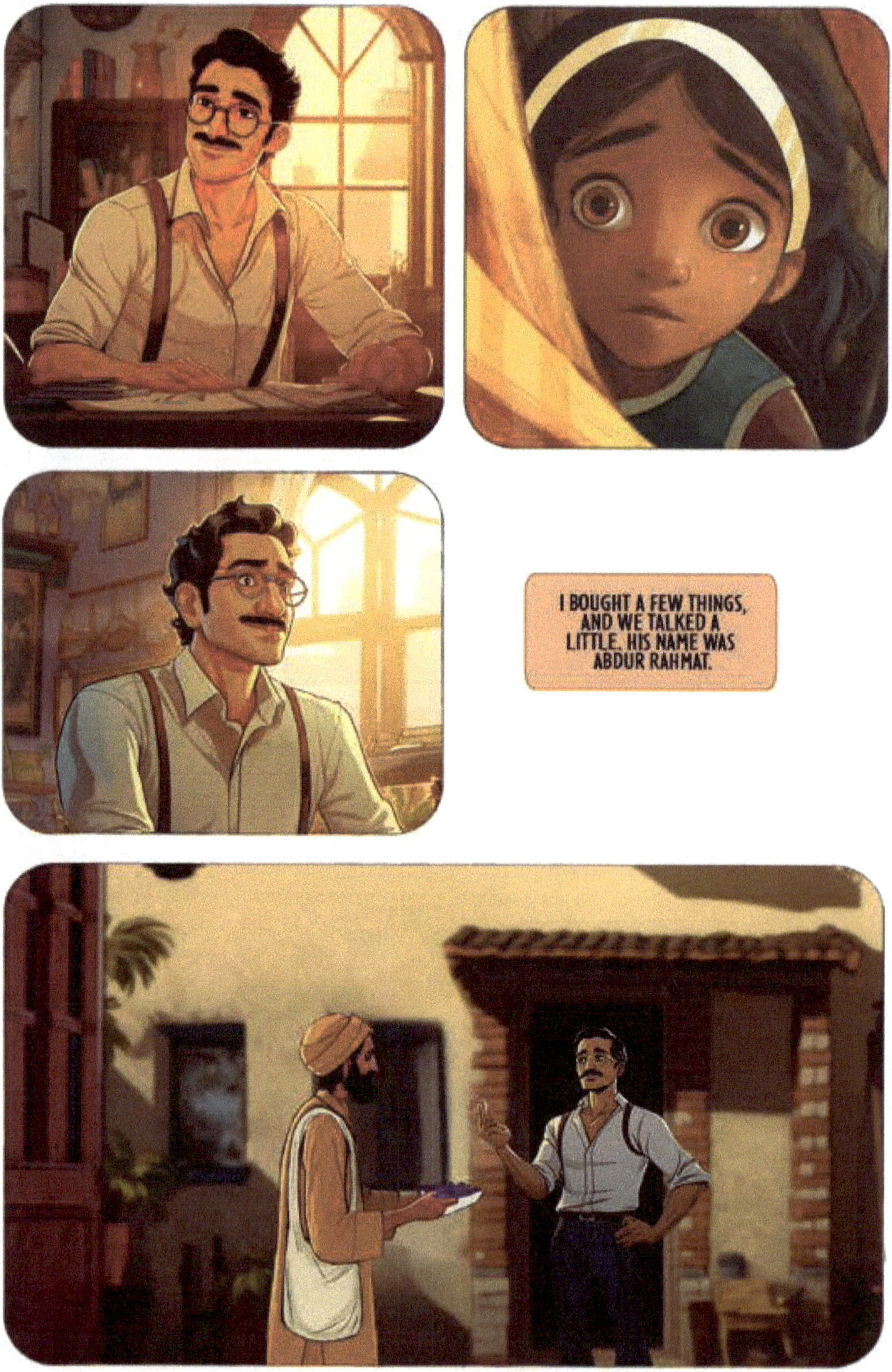
I BOUGHT A FEW THINGS, AND WE TALKED A LITTLE. HIS NAME WAS ABDUR RAHMAT.

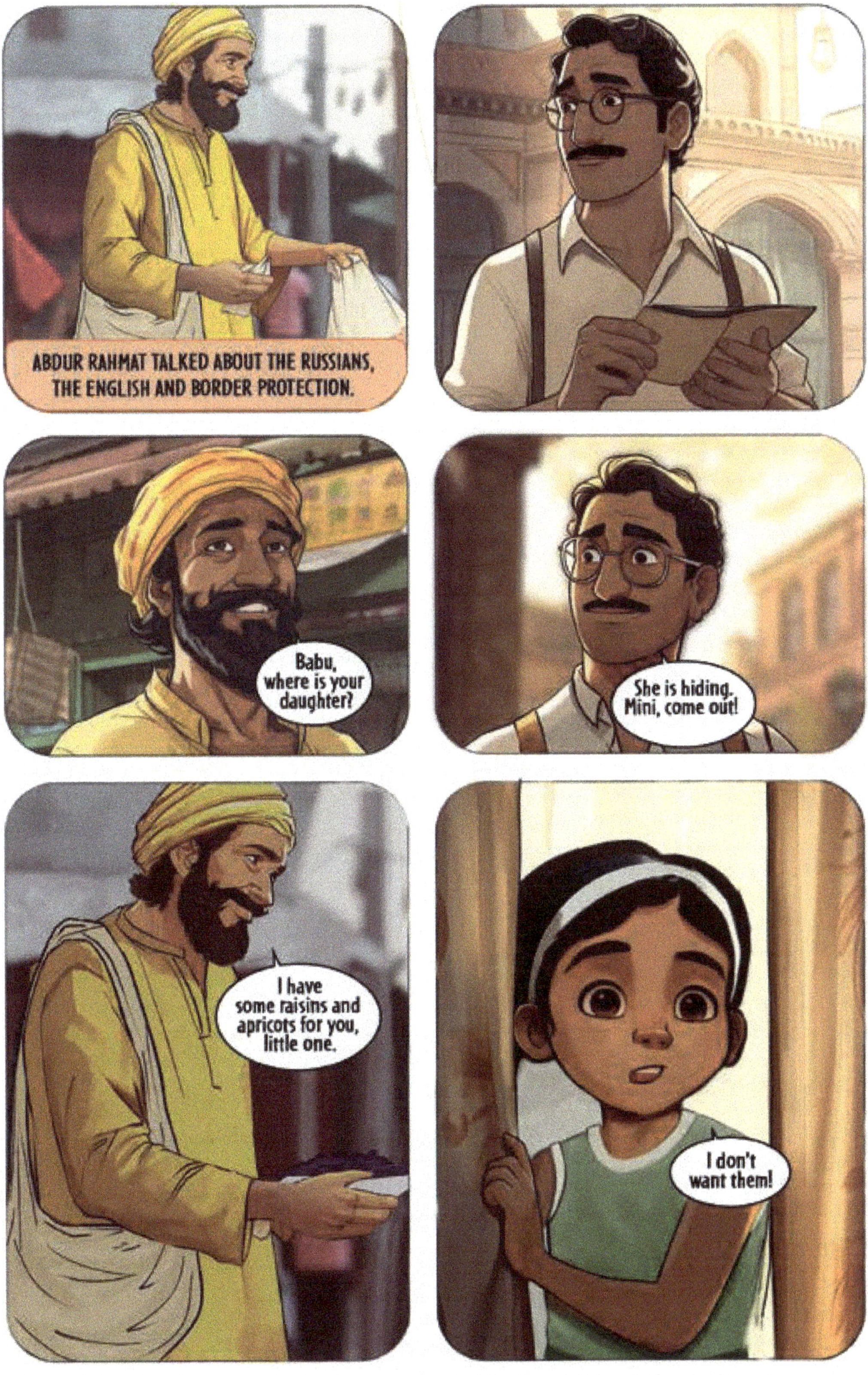
ABDUR RAHMAT TALKED ABOUT THE RUSSIANS, THE ENGLISH AND BORDER PROTECTION.
Babu, where is your daughter?
She is hiding. Mini, come out!
I have some raisins and apricots for you, little one.
I don't want them!

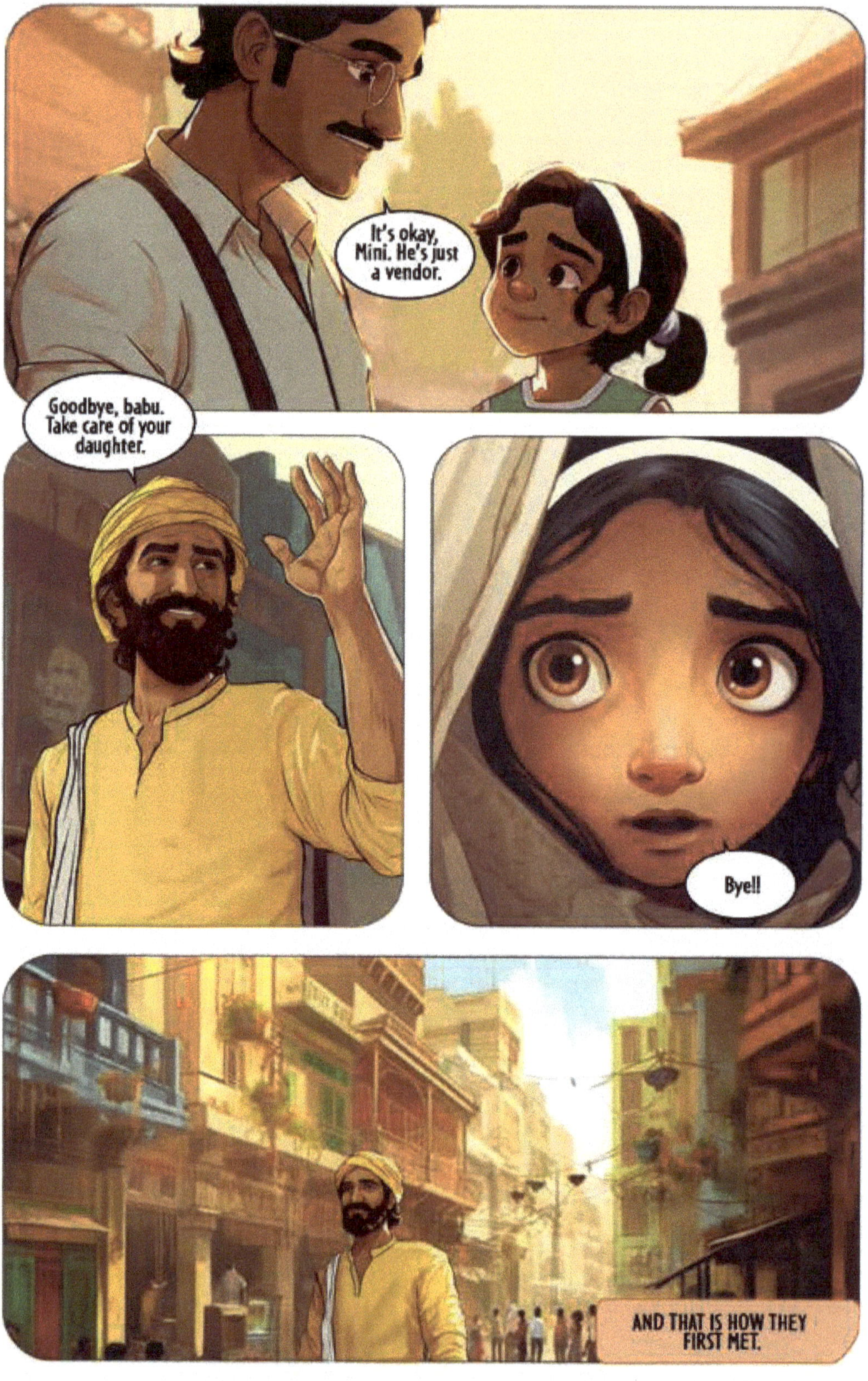
It's okay, Mini. He's just a vendor.
Goodbye, babu. Take care of your daughter.
Bye!!
AND THAT IS HOW THEY FIRST MET.

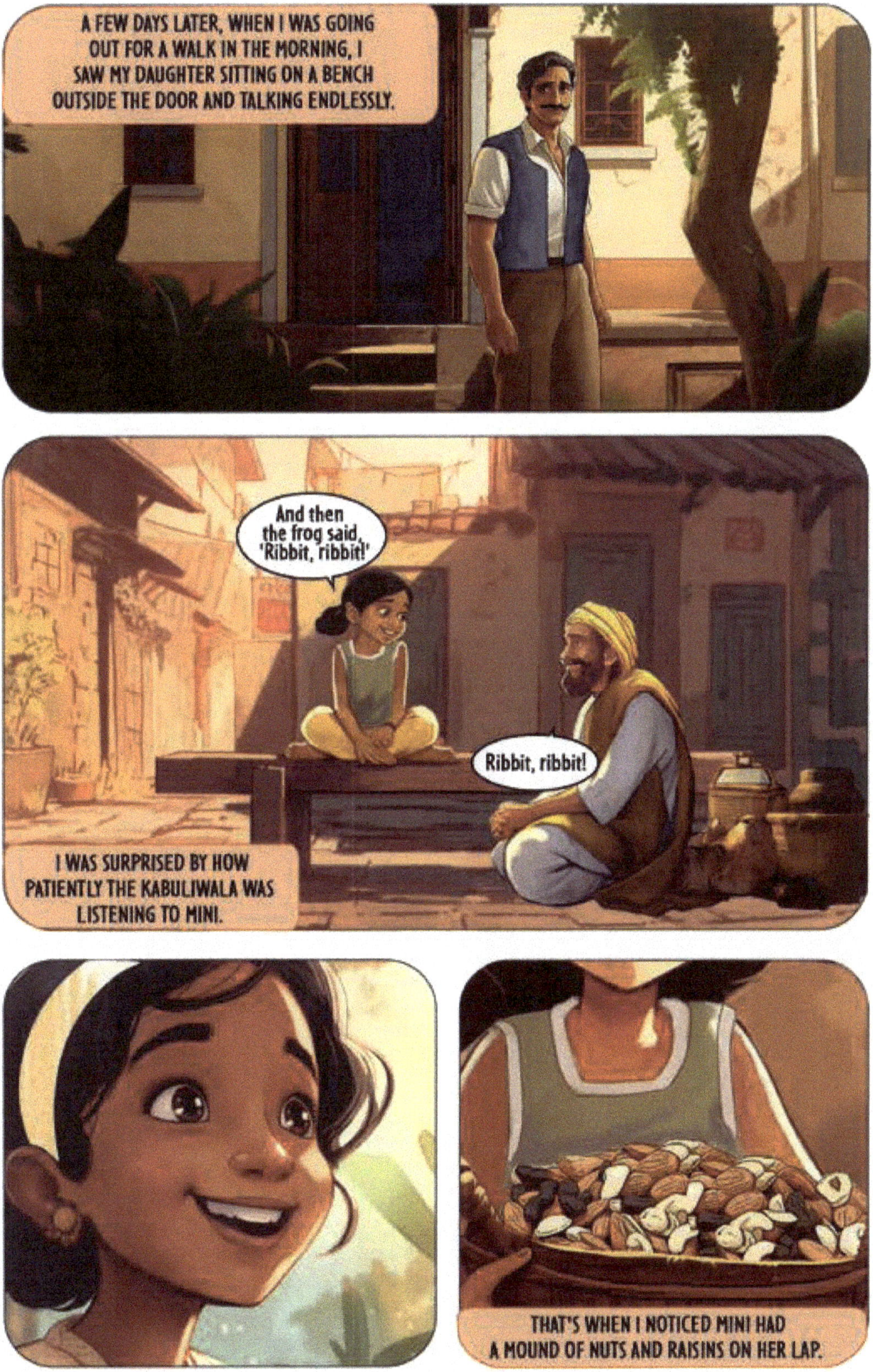
A FEW DAYS LATER, WHEN I WAS GOING OUT FOR A WALK IN THE MORNING, I SAW MY DAUGHTER SITTING ON A BENCH OUTSIDE THE DOOR AND TALKING ENDLESSLY.
And then the frog said, 'Ribbit, ribbit!'
Ribbit, ribbit!
I WAS SURPRISED BY HOW PATIENTLY THE KABULIWALA WAS LISTENING TO MINI.
THAT'S WHEN I NOTICED MINI HAD A MOUND OF NUTS AND RAISINS ON HER LAP.

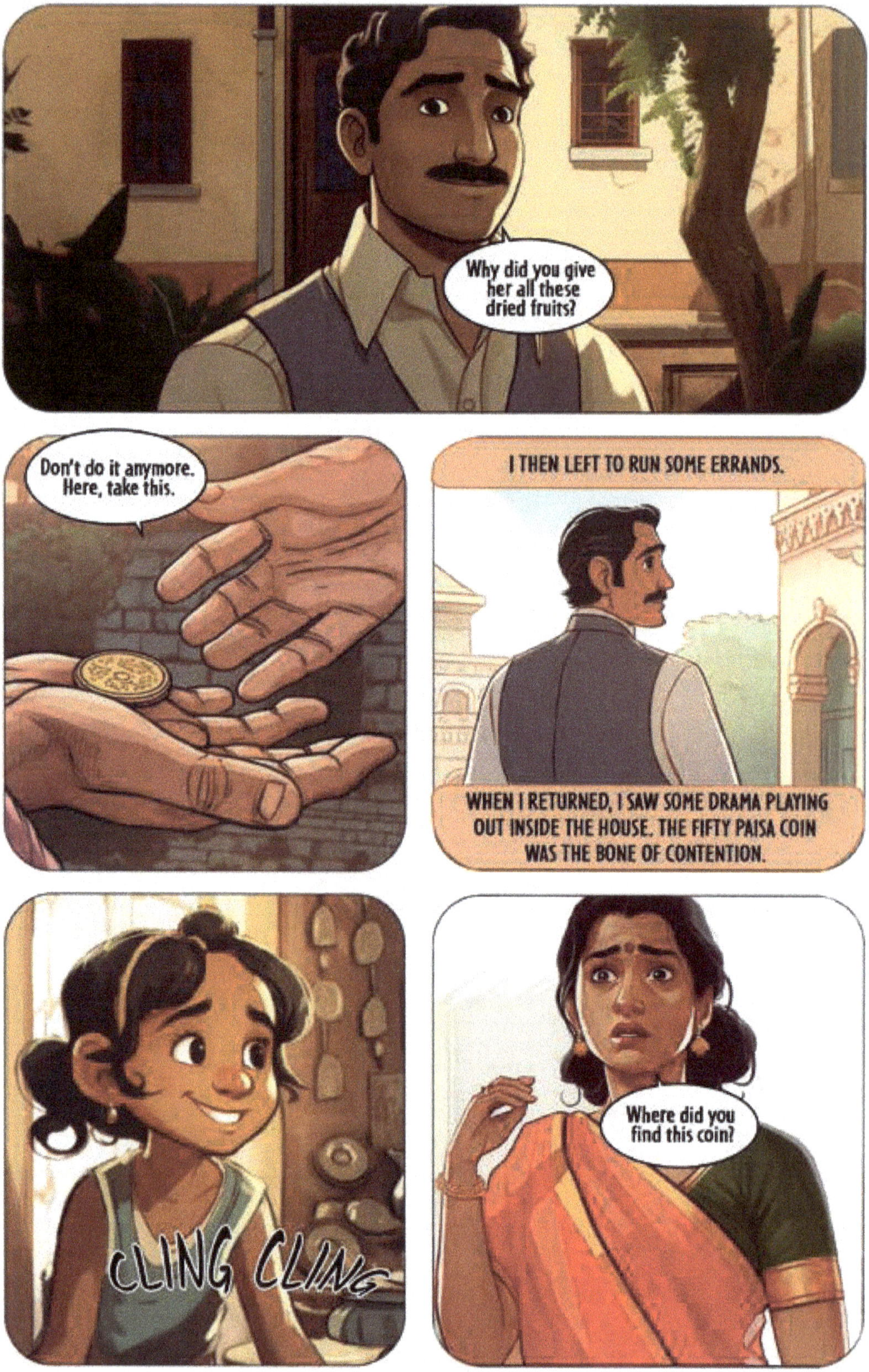
Why did you give her all these dried fruits?
Don't do it anymore. Here, take this.
I THEN LEFT TO RUN SOME ERRANDS.
WHEN I RETURNED, I SAW SOME DRAMA PLAYING OUT INSIDE THE HOUSE. THE FIFTY PAISA COIN WAS THE BONE OF CONTENTION.
CLING CLING
Where did you find this coin?

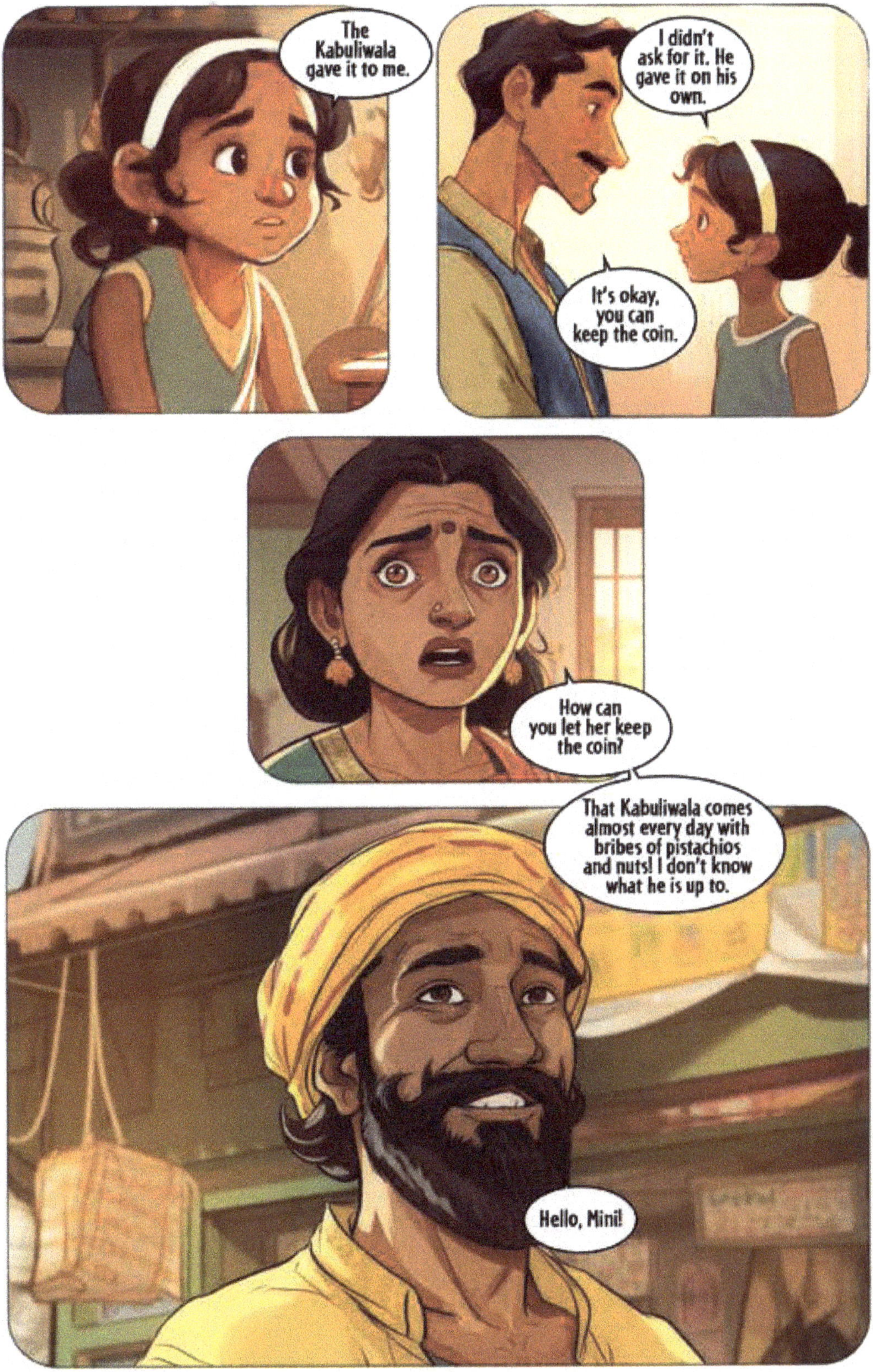
The Kabuliwala gave it to me.
I didn't ask for it. He gave it on his own.
It's okay, you can keep the coin.
How can you let her keep the coin?
That Kabuliwala comes almost every day with bribes of pistachios and nuts! I don't know what he is up to.
Hello, Mini!

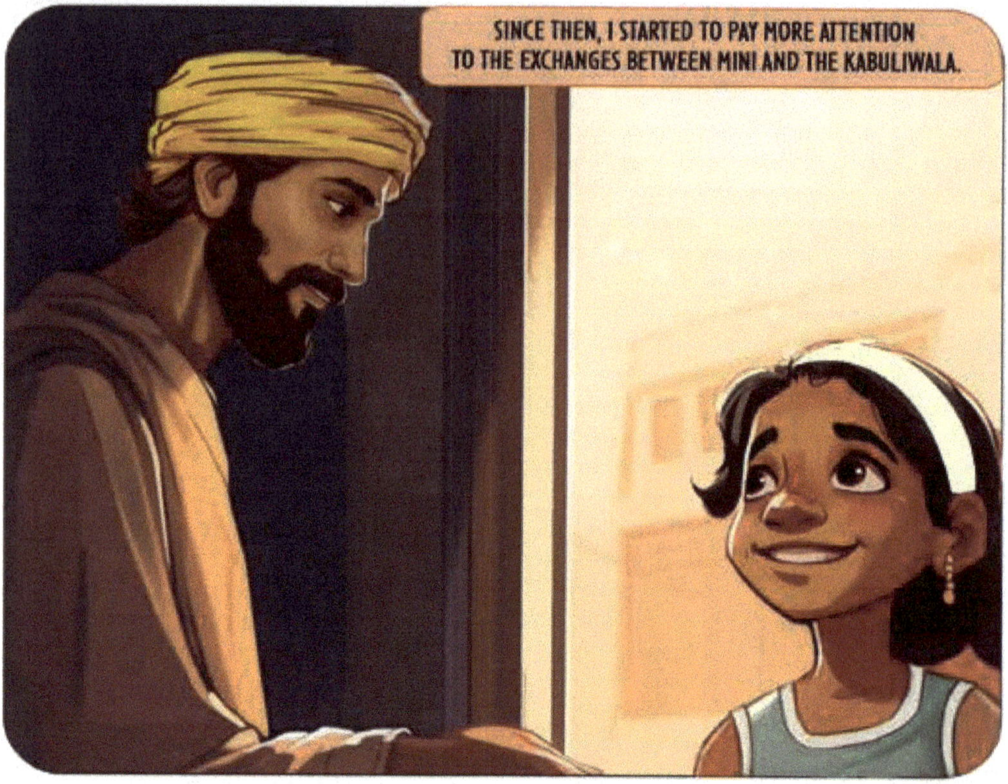
SINCE THEN, I STARTED TO PAY MORE ATTENTION TO THE EXCHANGES BETWEEN MINI AND THE KABULIWALA.

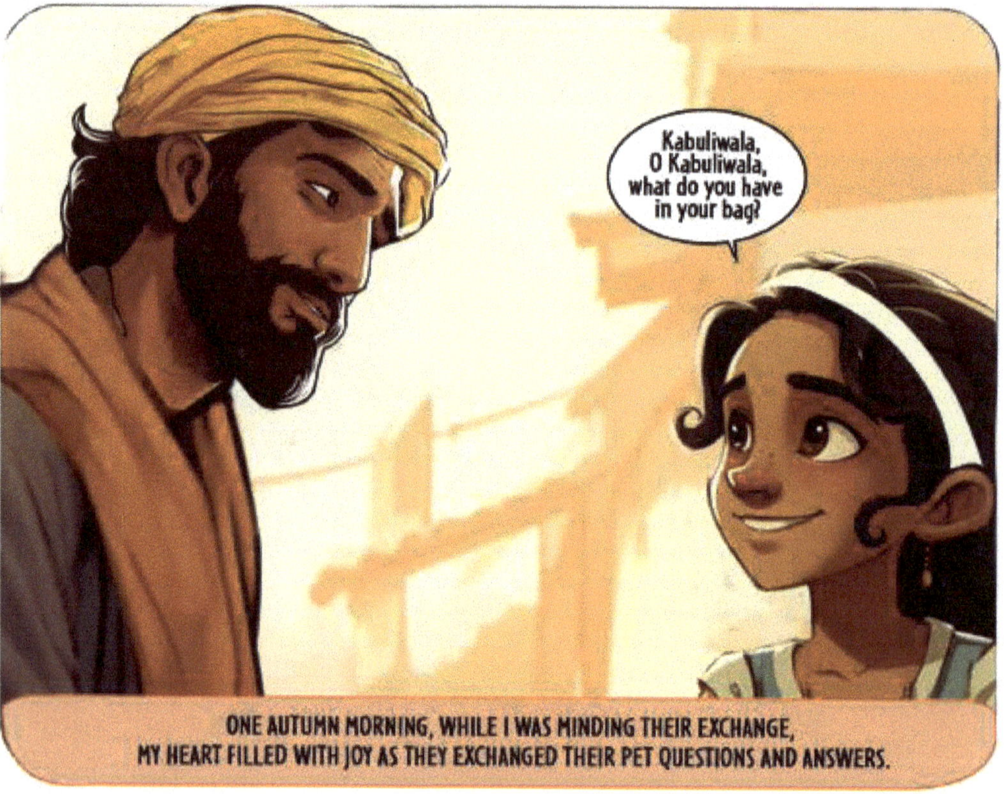
Kabuliwala, O Kabuliwala, what do you have in your bag?
ONE AUTUMN MORNING, WHILE I WAS MINDING THEIR EXCHANGE, MY HEART FILLED WITH JOY AS THEY EXCHANGED THEIR PET QUESTIONS AND ANSWERS.

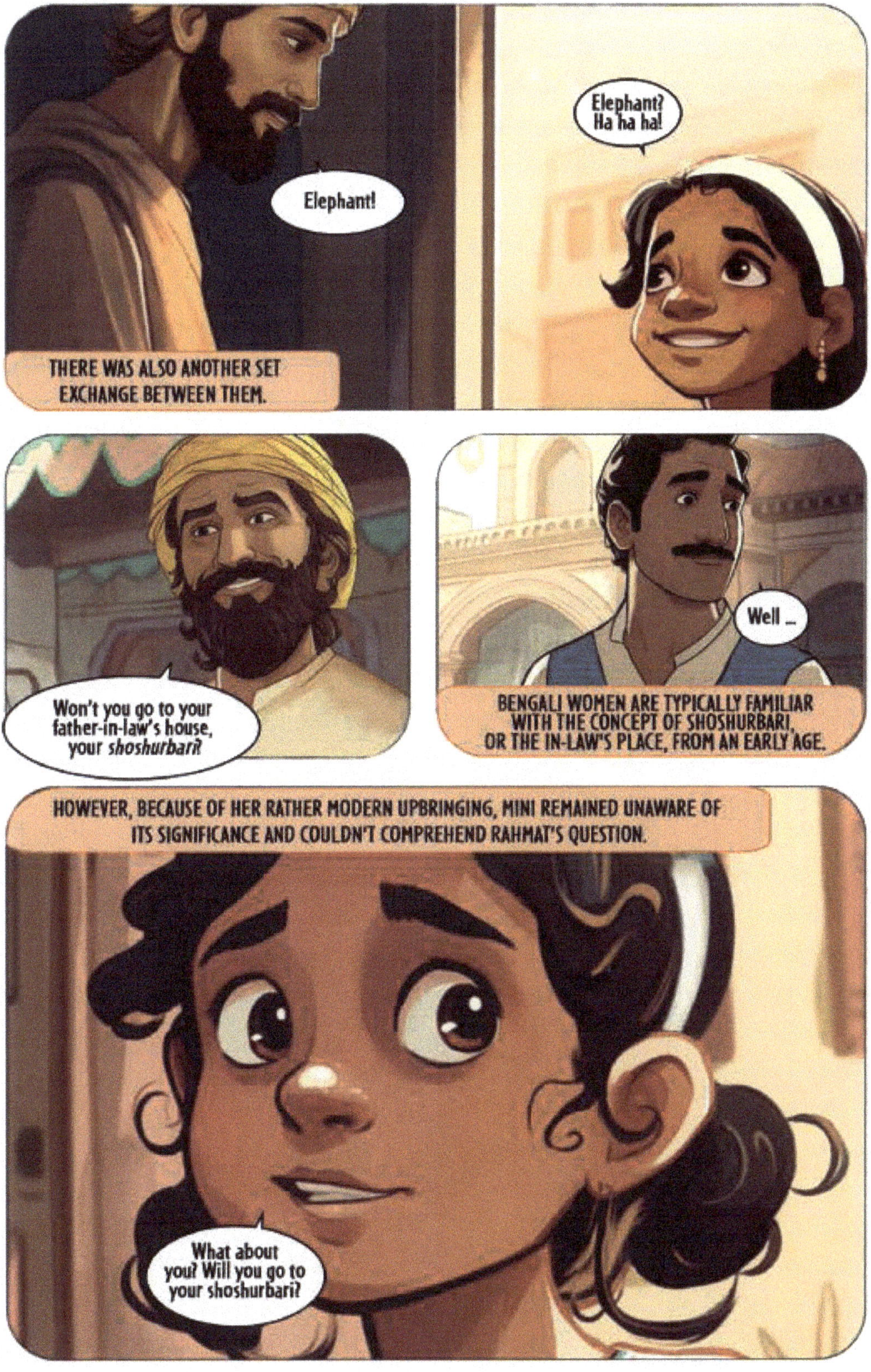
Elephant!
Elephant? Ha ha ha!
THERE WAS ALSO ANOTHER SET EXCHANGE BETWEEN THEM.
Won't you go to your father-in-law's house, your *shoshurbari*?
Well ...
BENGALI WOMEN ARE TYPICALLY FAMILIAR WITH THE CONCEPT OF SHOSHURBARI, OR THE IN-LAW'S PLACE, FROM AN EARLY AGE.
HOWEVER, BECAUSE OF HER RATHER MODERN UPBRINGING, MINI REMAINED UNAWARE OF ITS SIGNIFICANCE AND COULDN'T COMPREHEND RAHMAT'S QUESTION.
What about you? Will you go to your shoshurbari?

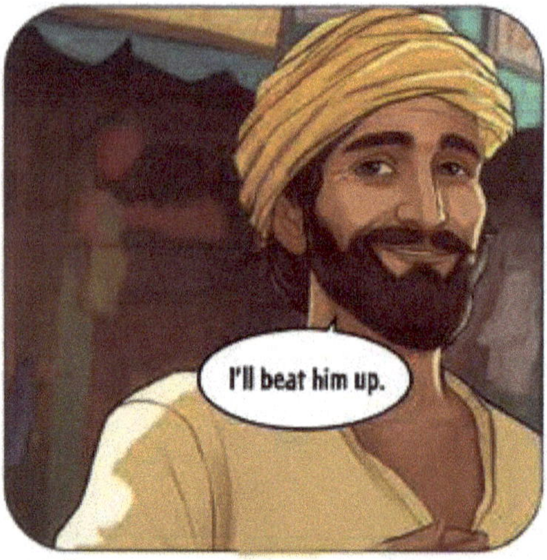
I'll beat him up.

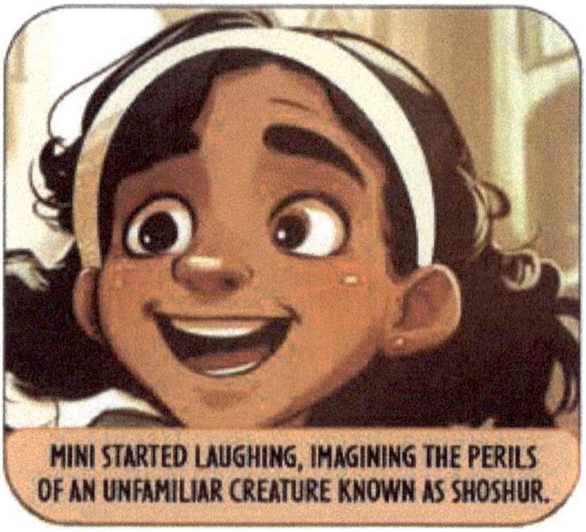
MINI STARTED LAUGHING, IMAGINING THE PERILS OF AN UNFAMILIAR CREATURE KNOWN AS SHOSHUR.

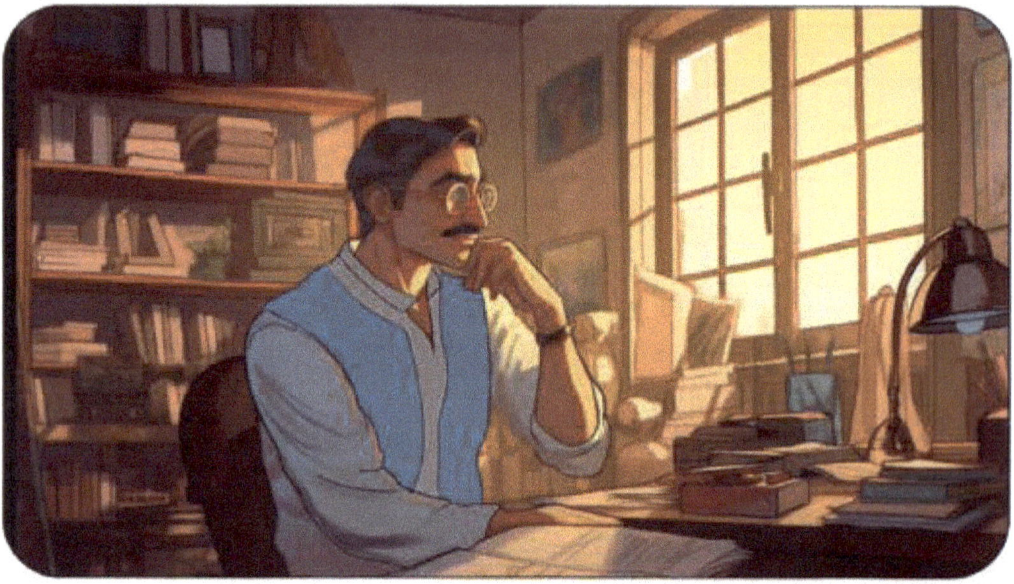

IT WAS AUTUMN. A TIME WHEN KINGS WOULD VENTURE FORTH TO CONQUER NEW LANDS, IN ANCIENT TIMES.

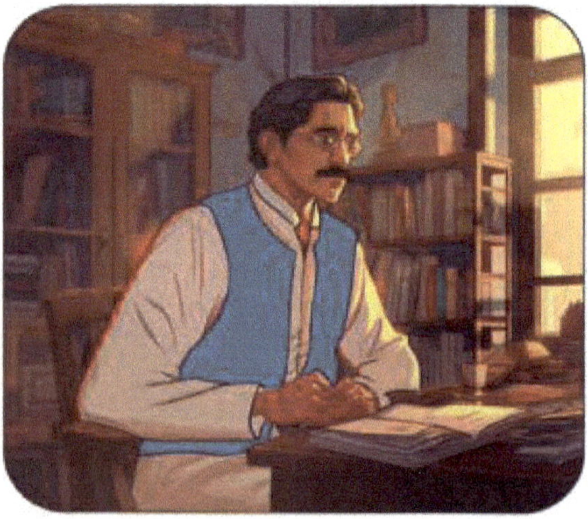

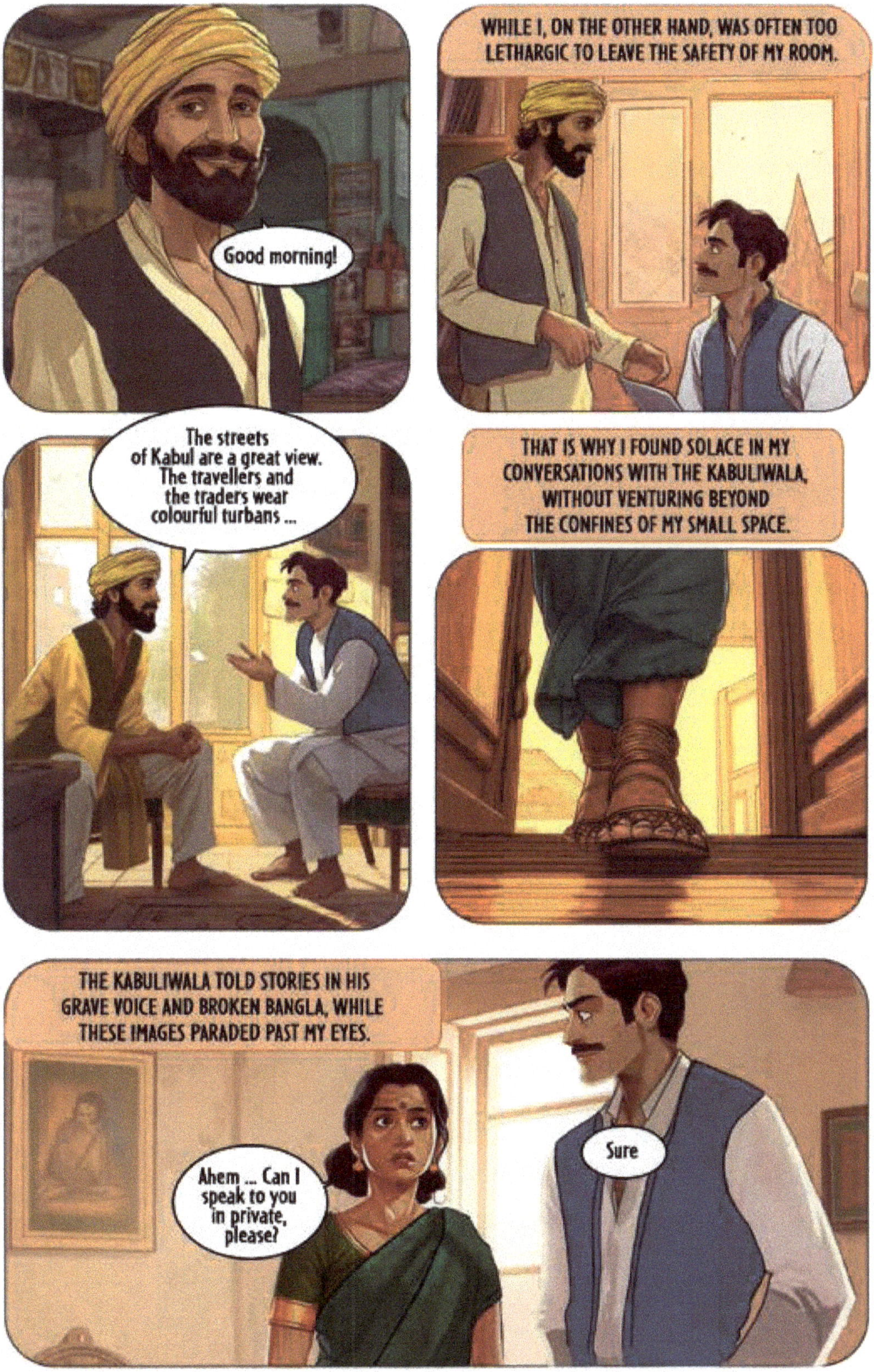
Good morning!
WHILE I, ON THE OTHER HAND, WAS OFTEN TOO LETHARGIC TO LEAVE THE SAFETY OF MY ROOM.
The streets of Kabul are a great view. The travellers and the traders wear colourful turbans ...
THAT IS WHY I FOUND SOLACE IN MY CONVERSATIONS WITH THE KABULIWALA, WITHOUT VENTURING BEYOND THE CONFINES OF MY SMALL SPACE.
THE KABULIWALA TOLD STORIES IN HIS GRAVE VOICE AND BROKEN BANGLA, WHILE THESE IMAGES PARADED PAST MY EYES.
Ahem ... Can I speak to you in private, please?
Sure

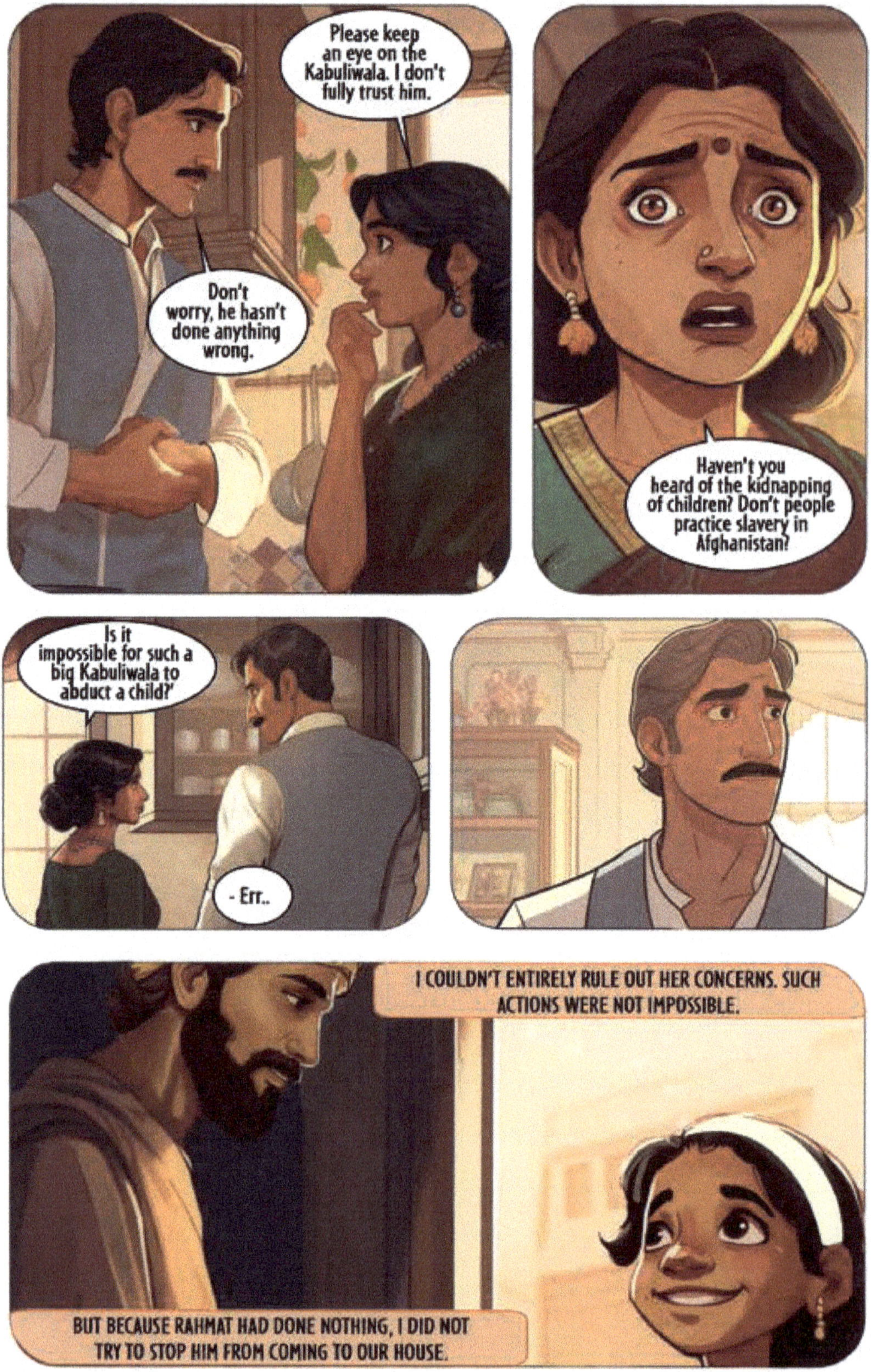

Please keep an eye on the Kabuliwala. I don't fully trust him.
Don't worry, he hasn't done anything wrong.
Haven't you heard of the kidnapping of children? Don't people practice slavery in Afghanistan?
Is it impossible for such a big Kabuliwala to abduct a child?'
- Err..
I COULDN'T ENTIRELY RULE OUT HER CONCERNS. SUCH ACTIONS WERE NOT IMPOSSIBLE.
BUT BECAUSE RAHMAT HAD DONE NOTHING, I DID NOT TRY TO STOP HIM FROM COMING TO OUR HOUSE.

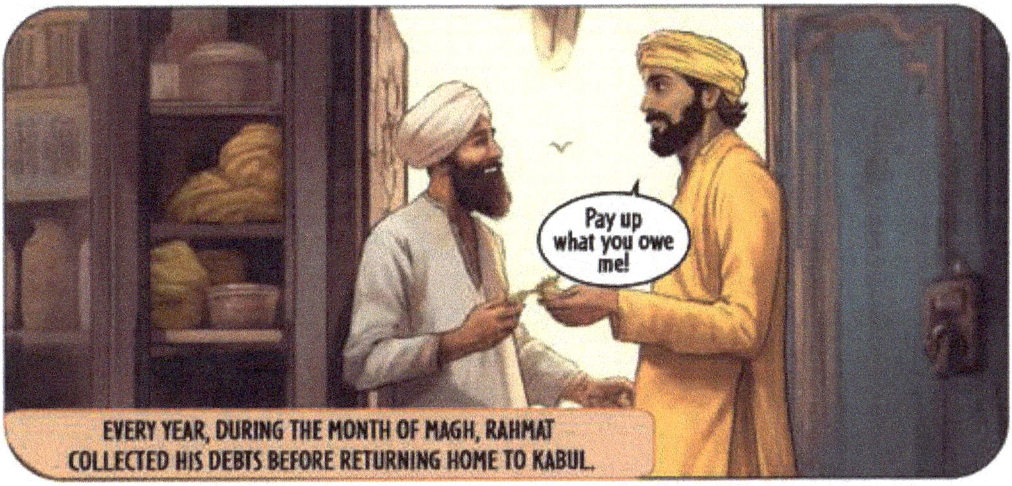
Pay up what you owe me!
EVERY YEAR, DURING THE MONTH OF MAGH, RAHMAT COLLECTED HIS DEBTS BEFORE RETURNING HOME TO KABUL.

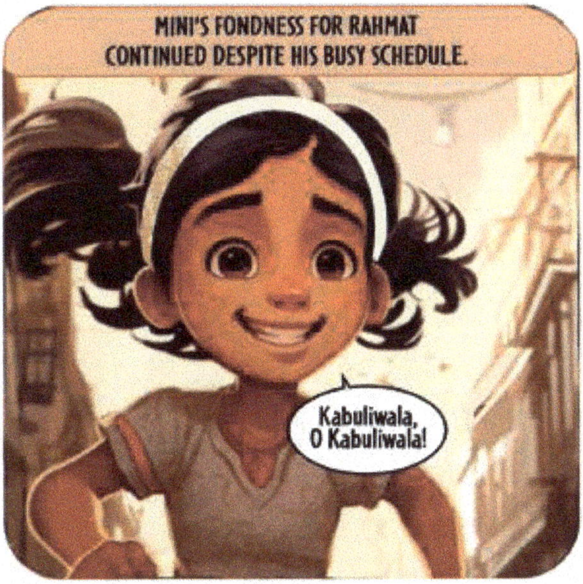
MINI'S FONDNESS FOR RAHMAT CONTINUED DESPITE HIS BUSY SCHEDULE.
Kabuliwala, O Kabuliwala!

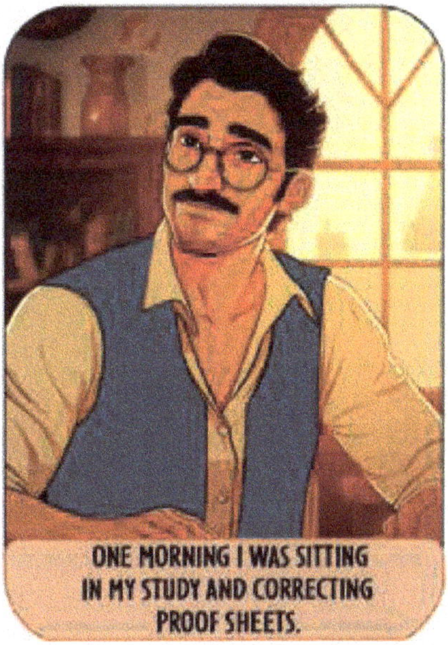
ONE MORNING I WAS SITTING IN MY STUDY AND CORRECTING PROOF SHEETS.

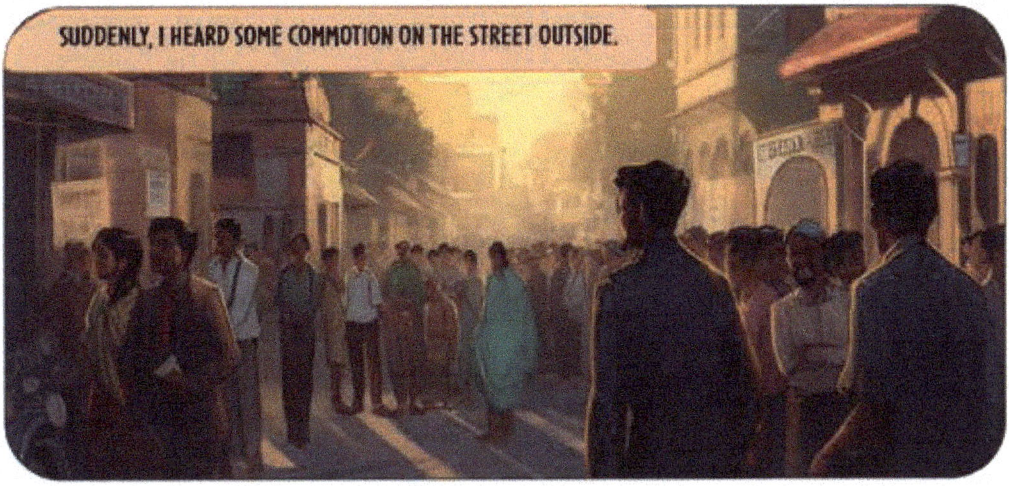
SUDDENLY, I HEARD SOME COMMOTION ON THE STREET OUTSIDE.

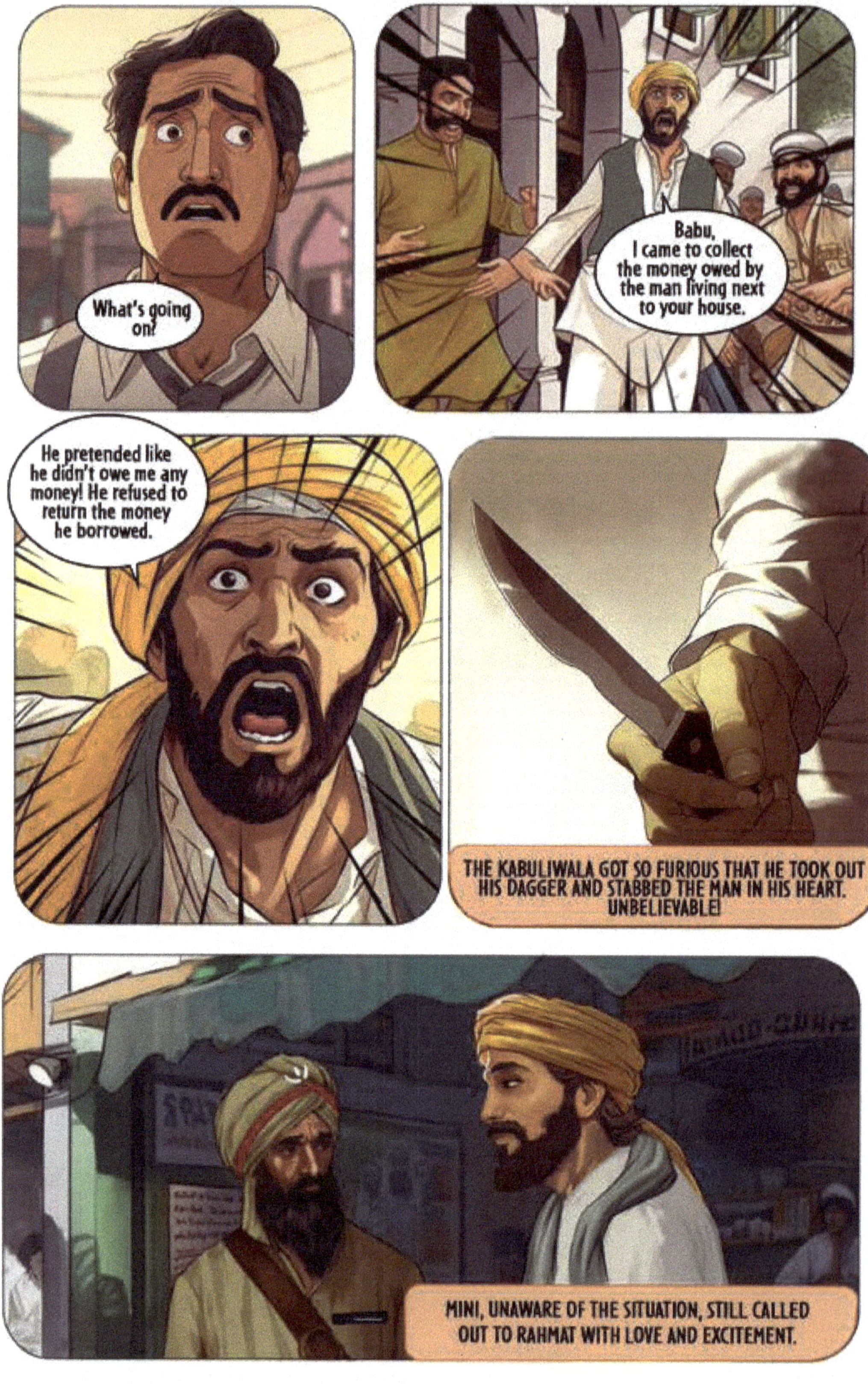
What's going on?
Babu, I came to collect the money owed by the man living next to your house.
He pretended like he didn't owe me any money! He refused to return the money he borrowed.
THE KABULIWALA GOT SO FURIOUS THAT HE TOOK OUT HIS DAGGER AND STABBED THE MAN IN HIS HEART. UNBELIEVABLE!
MINI, UNAWARE OF THE SITUATION, STILL CALLED OUT TO RAHMAT WITH LOVE AND EXCITEMENT.

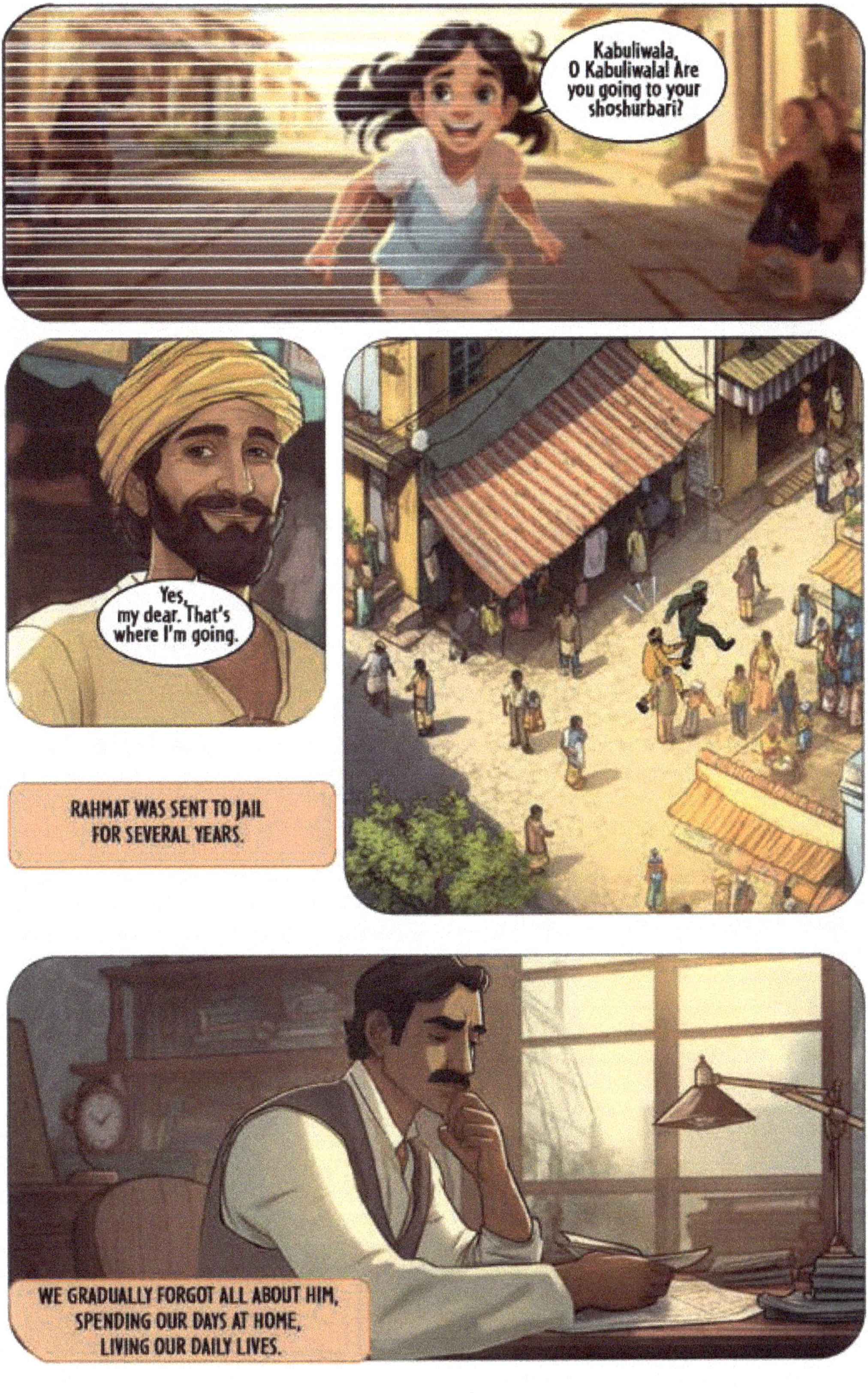
Kabuliwala, O Kabuliwala! Are you going to your shoshurbari?
Yes, my dear. That's where I'm going.
RAHMAT WAS SENT TO JAIL FOR SEVERAL YEARS.
WE GRADUALLY FORGOT ALL ABOUT HIM, SPENDING OUR DAYS AT HOME, LIVING OUR DAILY LIVES.

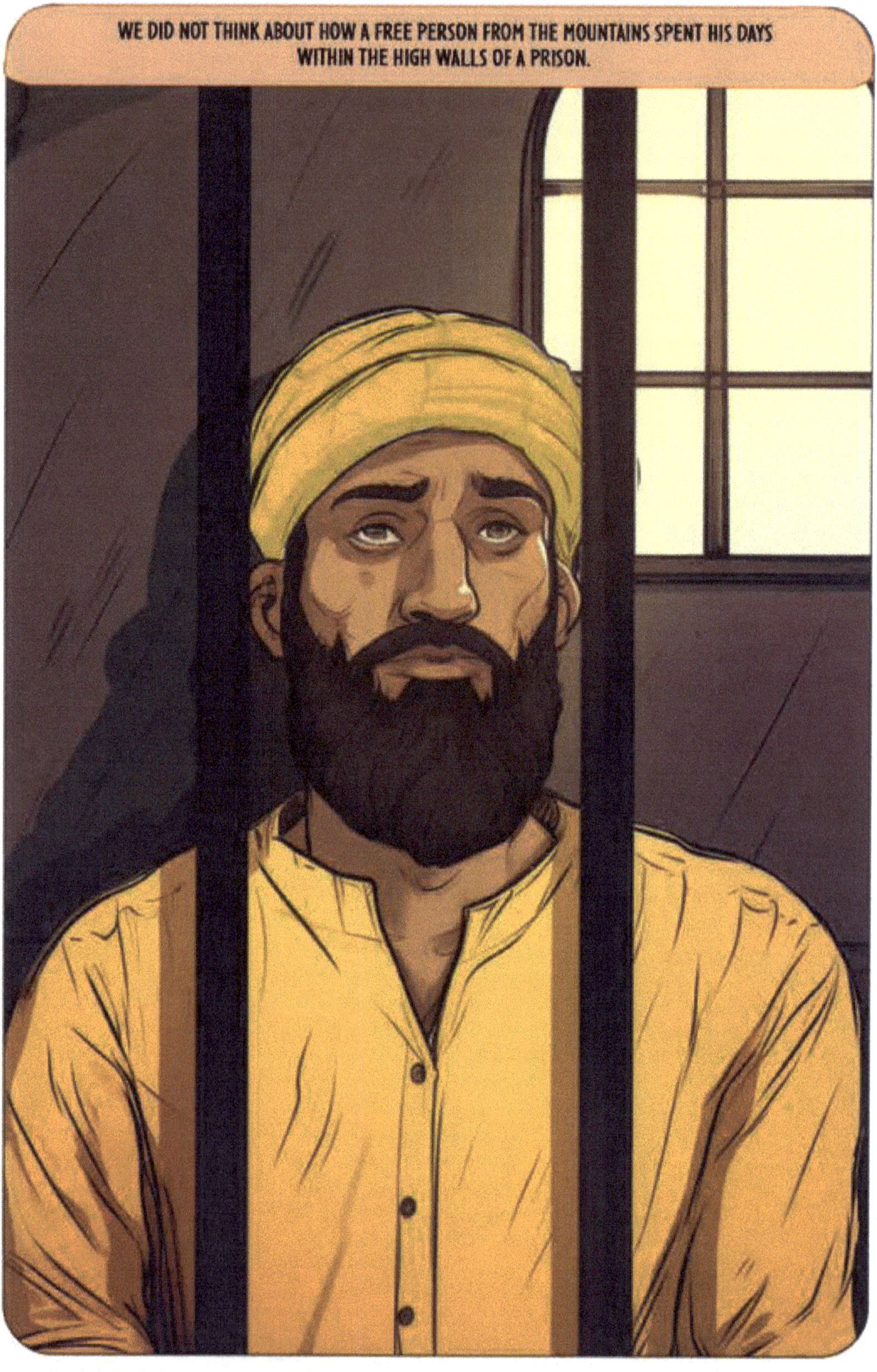
WE DID NOT THINK ABOUT HOW A FREE PERSON FROM THE MOUNTAINS SPENT HIS DAYS WITHIN THE HIGH WALLS OF A PRISON.

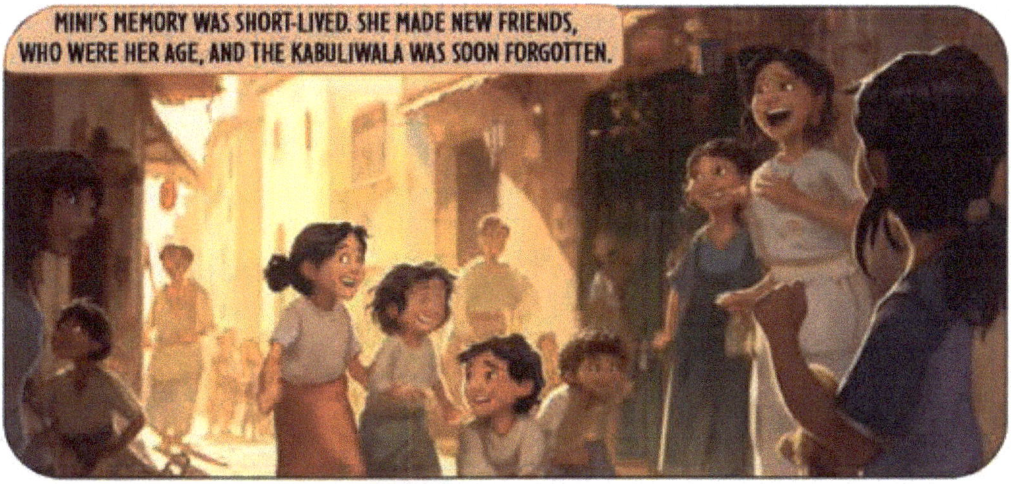
MINI'S MEMORY WAS SHORT-LIVED. SHE MADE NEW FRIENDS, WHO WERE HER AGE, AND THE KABULIWALA WAS SOON FORGOTTEN.

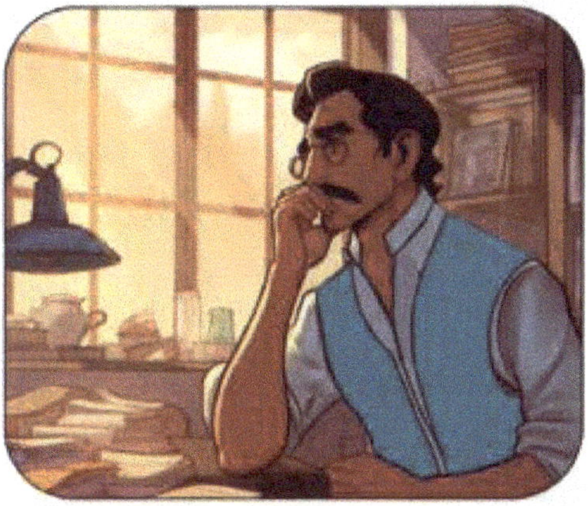

SHE STOPPED COMING TO MY DESK. I, TOO, FELT SOMEWHAT ABANDONED BY HER.

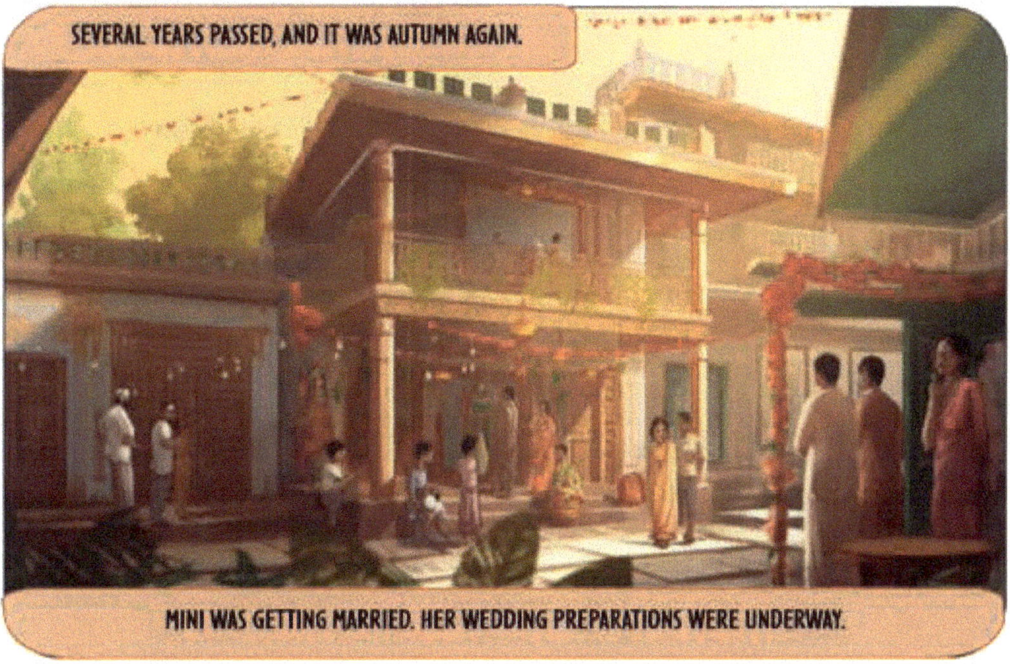
SEVERAL YEARS PASSED, AND IT WAS AUTUMN AGAIN.
MINI WAS GETTING MARRIED. HER WEDDING PREPARATIONS WERE UNDERWAY.

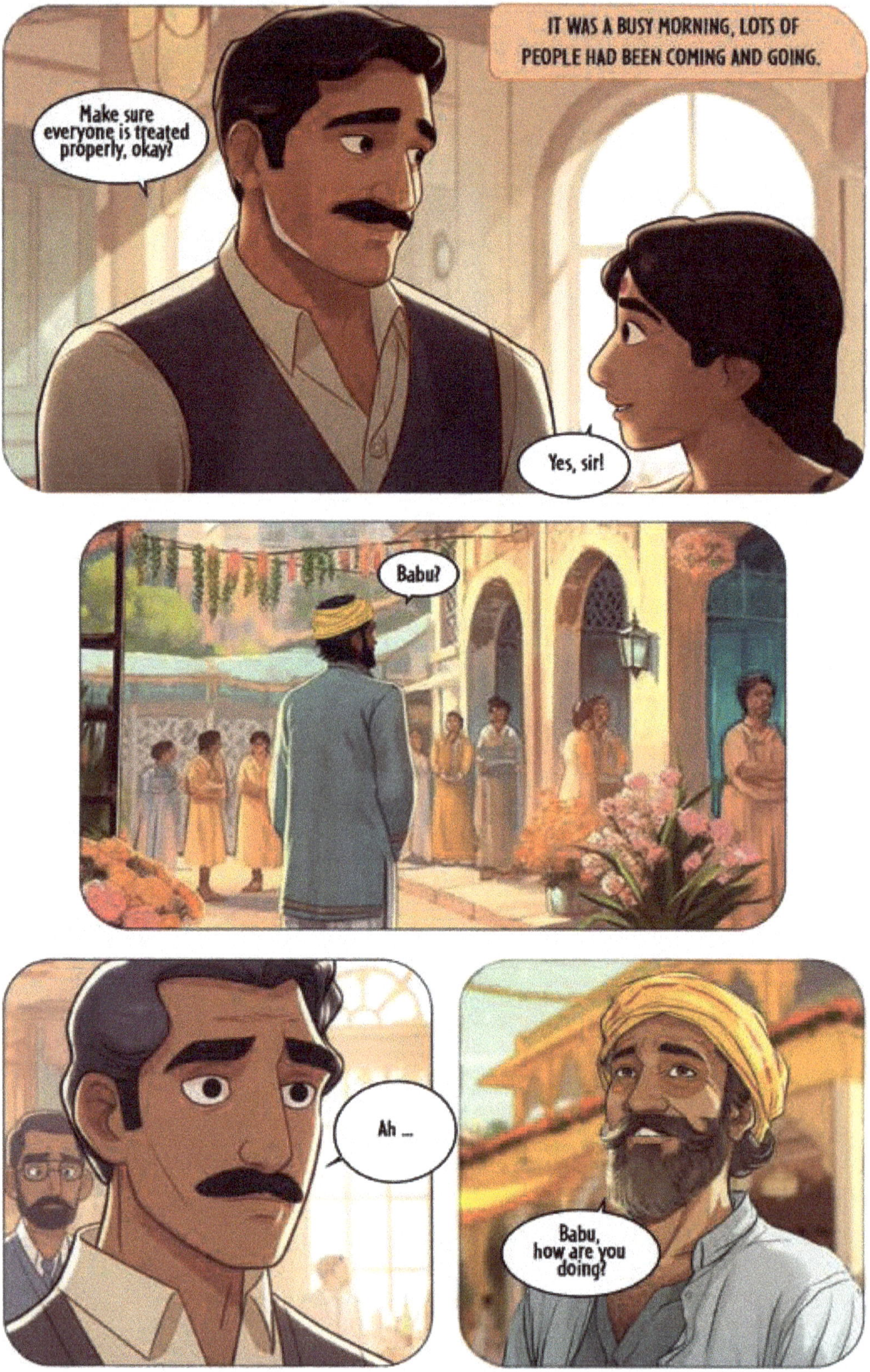
IT WAS A BUSY MORNING, LOTS OF PEOPLE HAD BEEN COMING AND GOING.
Make sure everyone is treated properly, okay?
Yes, sir!
Babu?
Ah ...
Babu, how are you doing?

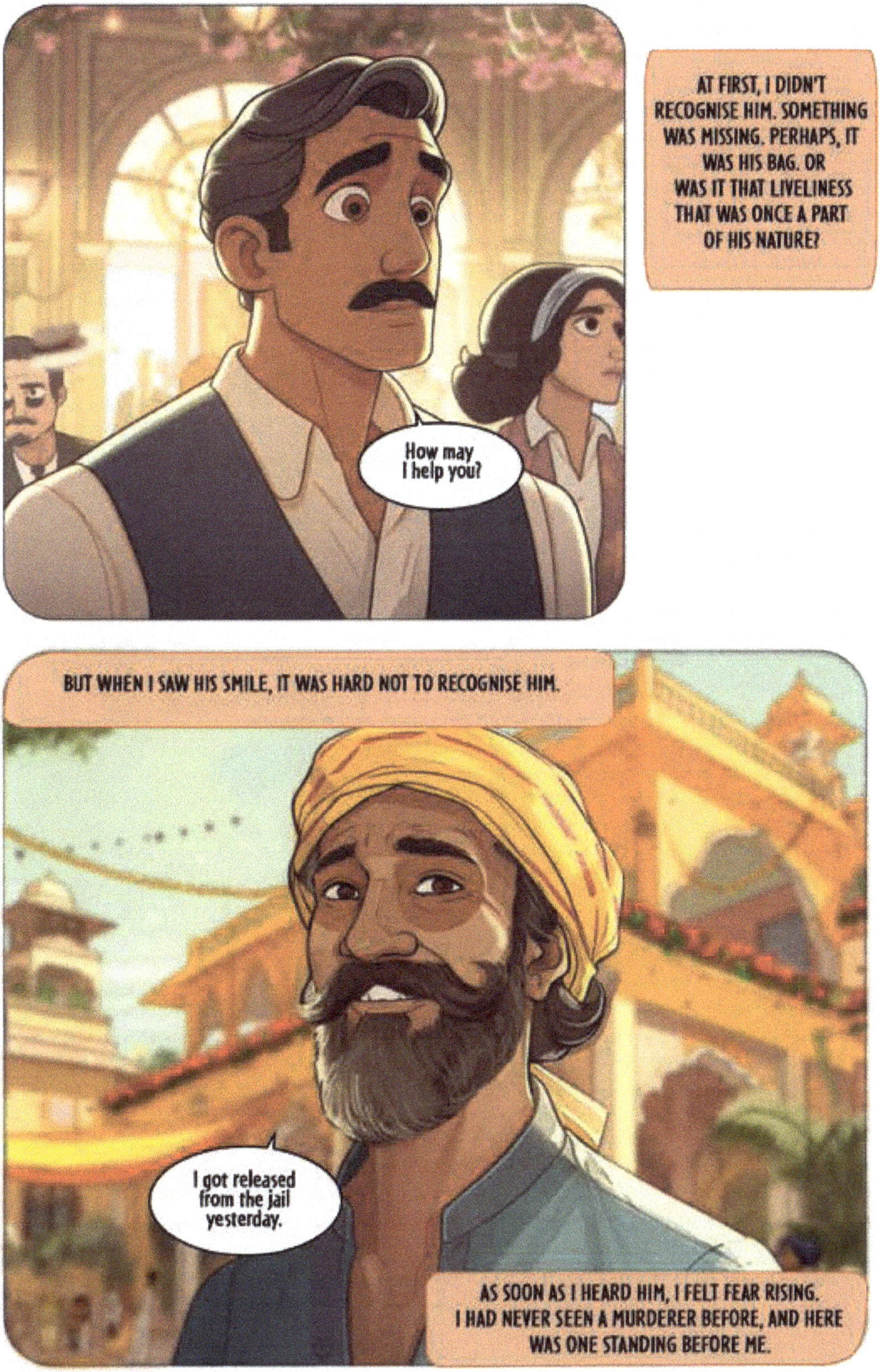
AT FIRST, I DIDN'T RECOGNISE HIM. SOMETHING WAS MISSING. PERHAPS, IT WAS HIS BAG. OR WAS IT THAT LIVELINESS THAT WAS ONCE A PART OF HIS NATURE?
How may I help you?
BUT WHEN I SAW HIS SMILE, IT WAS HARD NOT TO RECOGNISE HIM.
I got released from the jail yesterday.
AS SOON AS I HEARD HIM, I FELT FEAR RISING. I HAD NEVER SEEN A MURDERER BEFORE, AND HERE WAS ONE STANDING BEFORE ME.

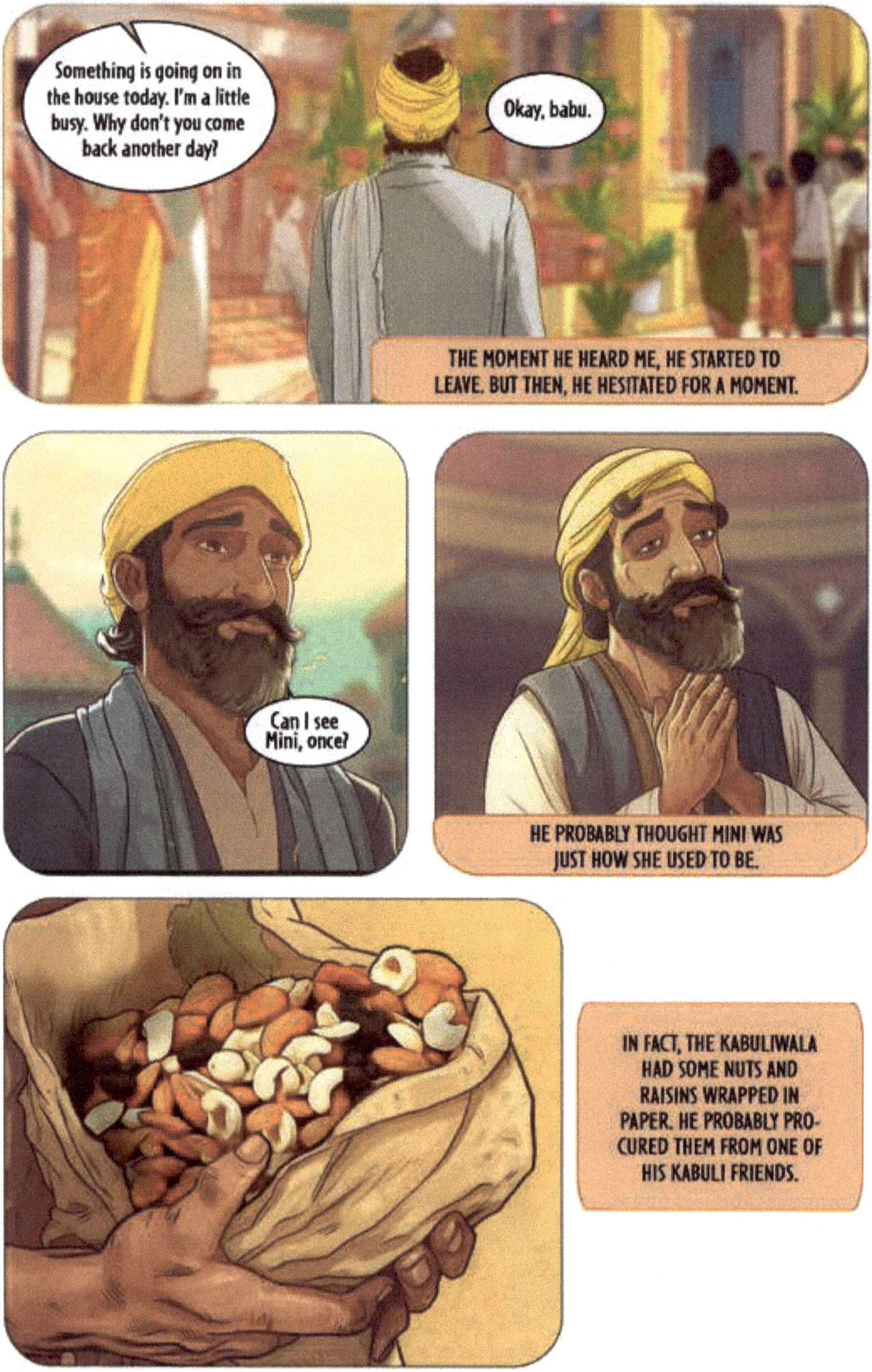
Something is going on in the house today. I'm a little busy. Why don't you come back another day?
Okay, babu.
THE MOMENT HE HEARD ME, HE STARTED TO LEAVE. BUT THEN, HE HESITATED FOR A MOMENT.
Can I see Mini, once?
HE PROBABLY THOUGHT MINI WAS JUST HOW SHE USED TO BE.
IN FACT, THE KABULIWALA HAD SOME NUTS AND RAISINS WRAPPED IN PAPER. HE PROBABLY PRO-CURED THEM FROM ONE OF HIS KABULI FRIENDS.

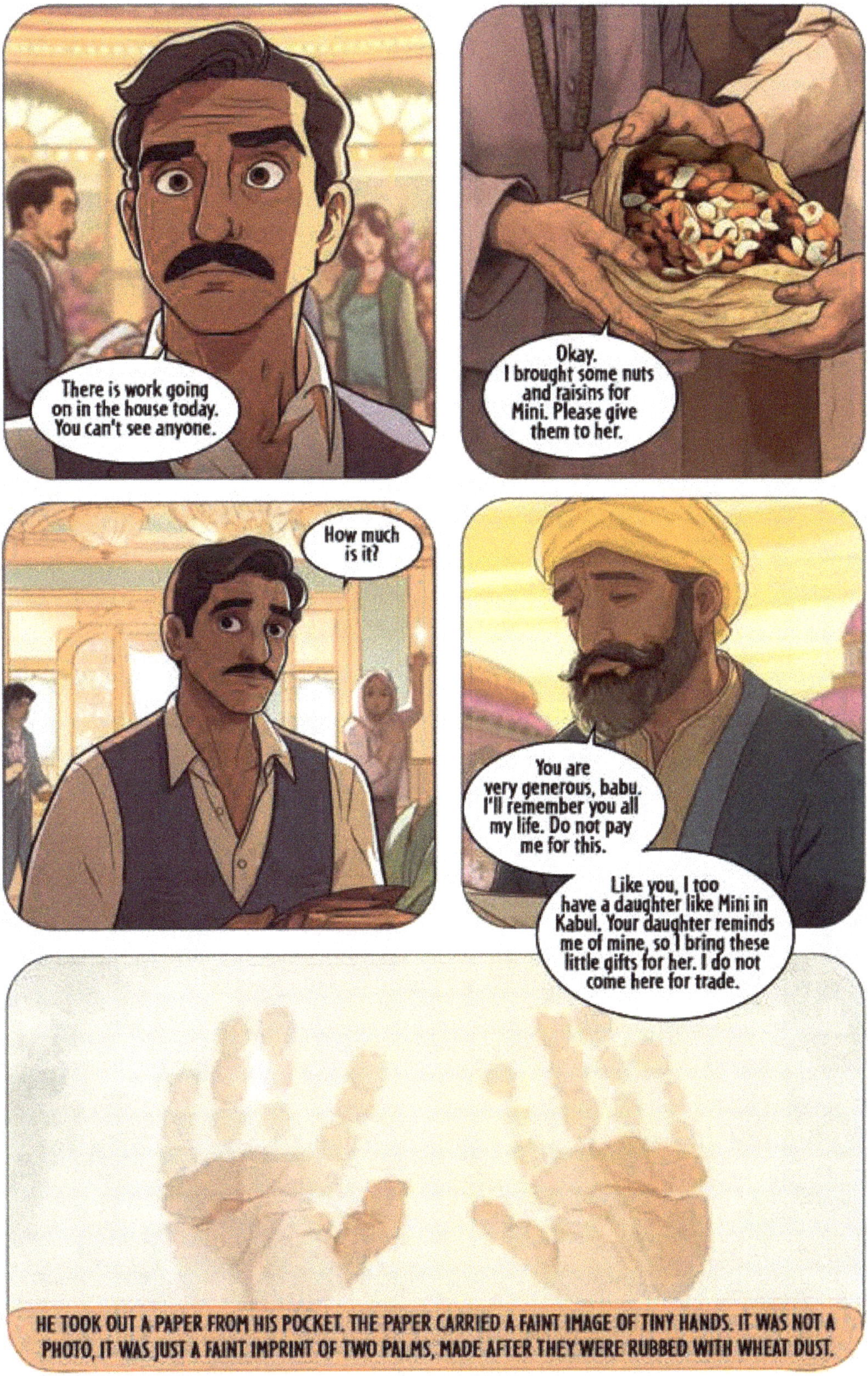
There is work going on in the house today. You can't see anyone.
Okay. I brought some nuts and raisins for Mini. Please give them to her.
How much is it?
You are very generous, babu. I'll remember you all my life. Do not pay me for this.
Like you, I too have a daughter like Mini in Kabul. Your daughter reminds me of mine, so I bring these little gifts for her. I do not come here for trade.
HE TOOK OUT A PAPER FROM HIS POCKET. THE PAPER CARRIED A FAINT IMAGE OF TINY HANDS. IT WAS NOT A PHOTO, IT WAS JUST A FAINT IMPRINT OF TWO PALMS, MADE AFTER THEY WERE RUBBED WITH WHEAT DUST.

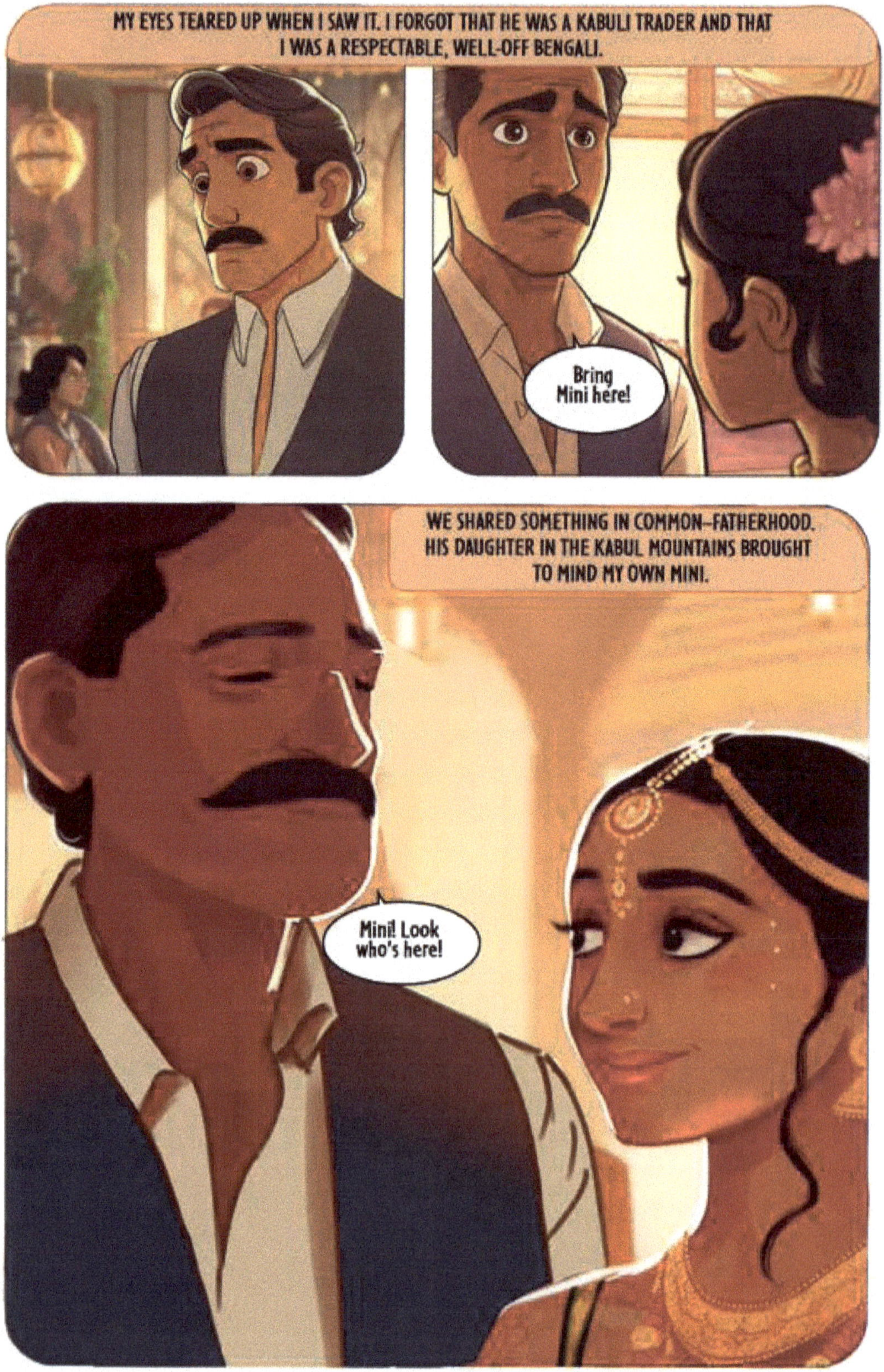

MY EYES TEARED UP WHEN I SAW IT. I FORGOT THAT HE WAS A KABULI TRADER AND THAT I WAS A RESPECTABLE, WELL-OFF BENGALI.
Bring Mini here!
WE SHARED SOMETHING IN COMMON–FATHERHOOD. HIS DAUGHTER IN THE KABUL MOUNTAINS BROUGHT TO MIND MY OWN MINI.
Mini! Look who's here!

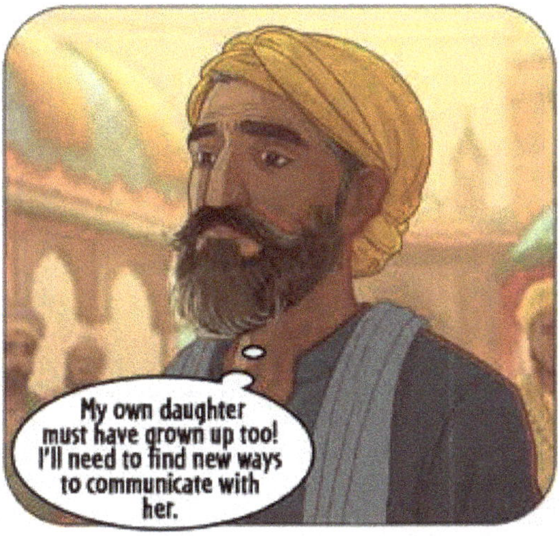
My own daughter must have grown up too! I'll need to find new ways to communicate with her.

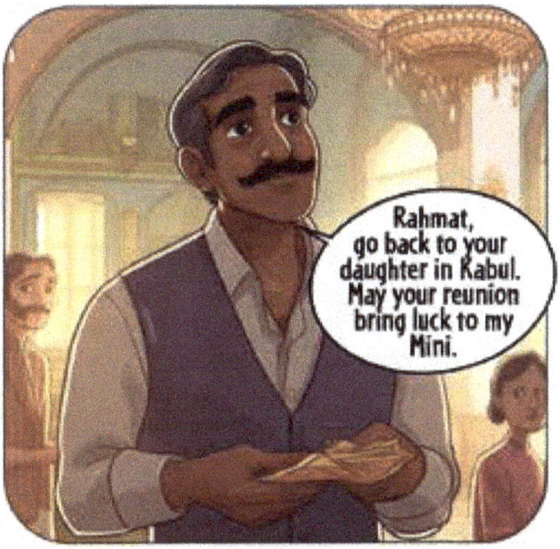
Rahmat, go back to your daughter in Kabul. May your reunion bring luck to my Mini.

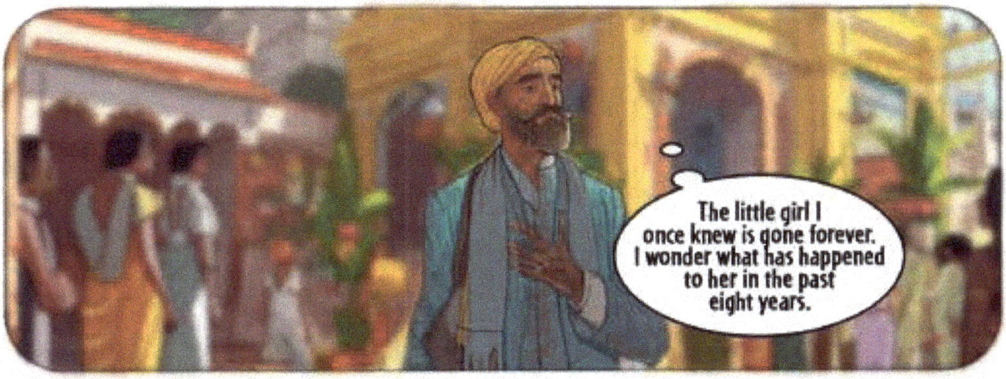
The little girl I once knew is gone forever. I wonder what has happened to her in the past eight years.

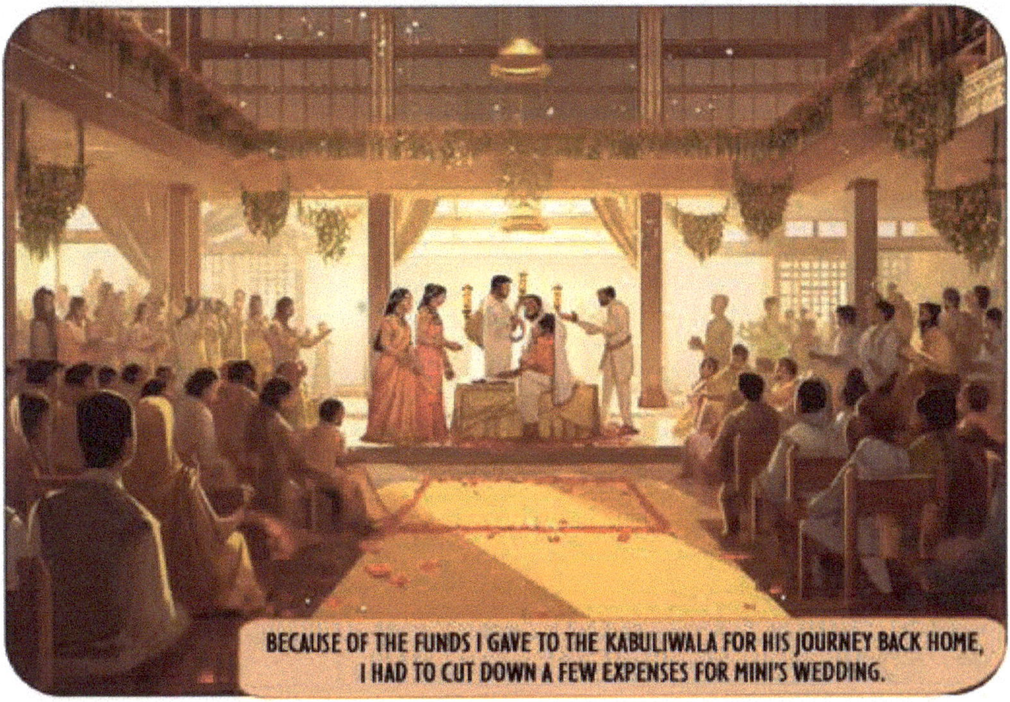
BECAUSE OF THE FUNDS I GAVE TO THE KABULIWALA FOR HIS JOURNEY BACK HOME, I HAD TO CUT DOWN A FEW EXPENSES FOR MINI'S WEDDING.

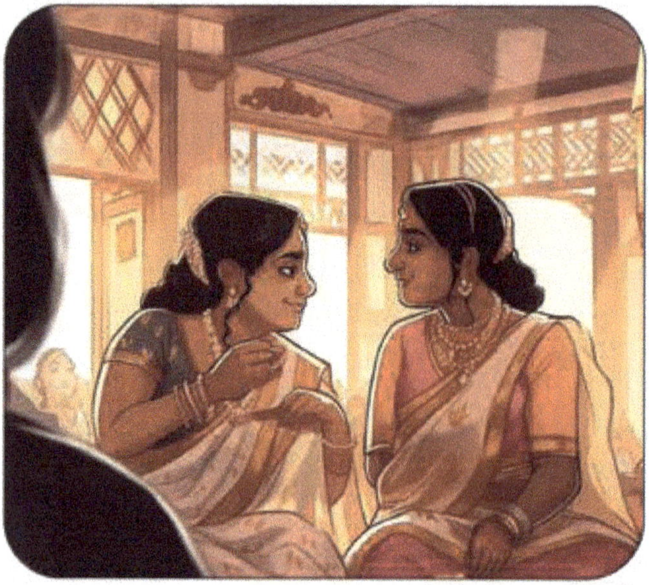

THE WOMEN INSIDE EXPRESSED THEIR DISSATISFACTION STRONGLY.

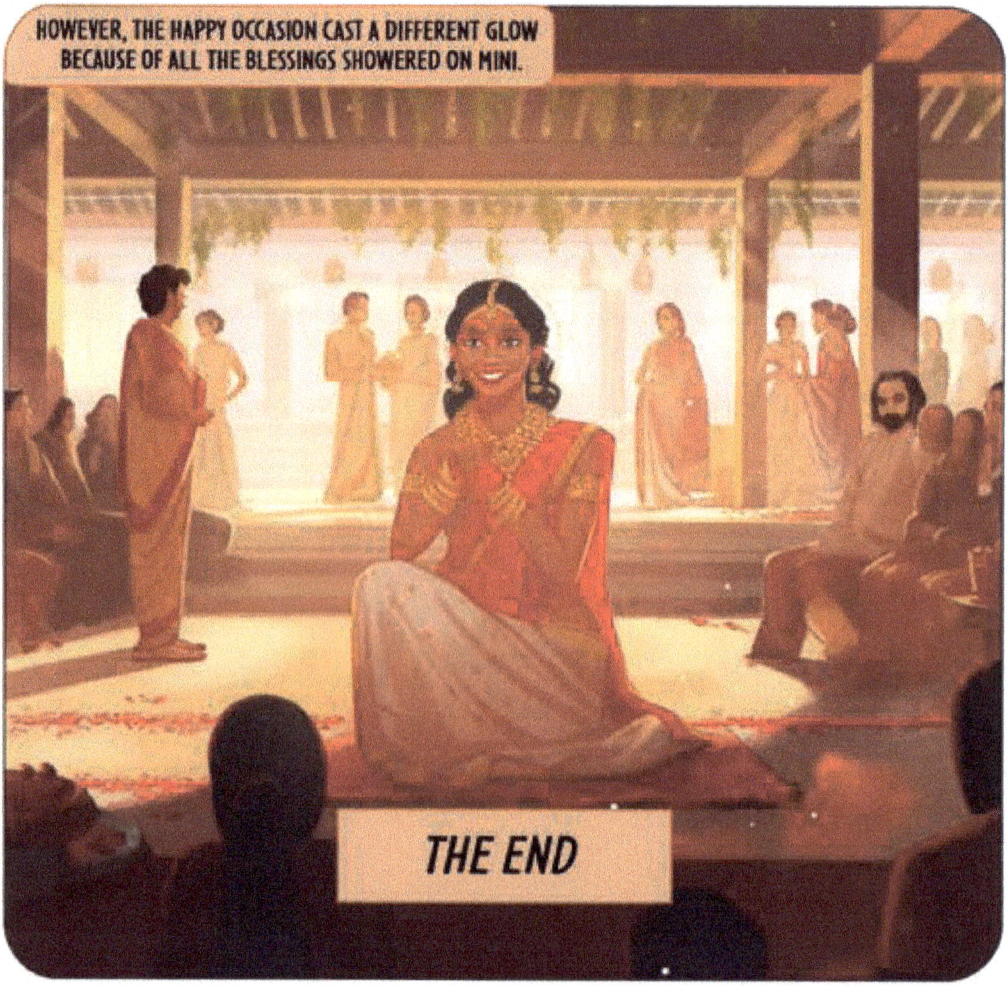
HOWEVER, THE HAPPY OCCASION CAST A DIFFERENT GLOW BECAUSE OF ALL THE BLESSINGS SHOWERED ON MINI.
THE END

POSTMASTER

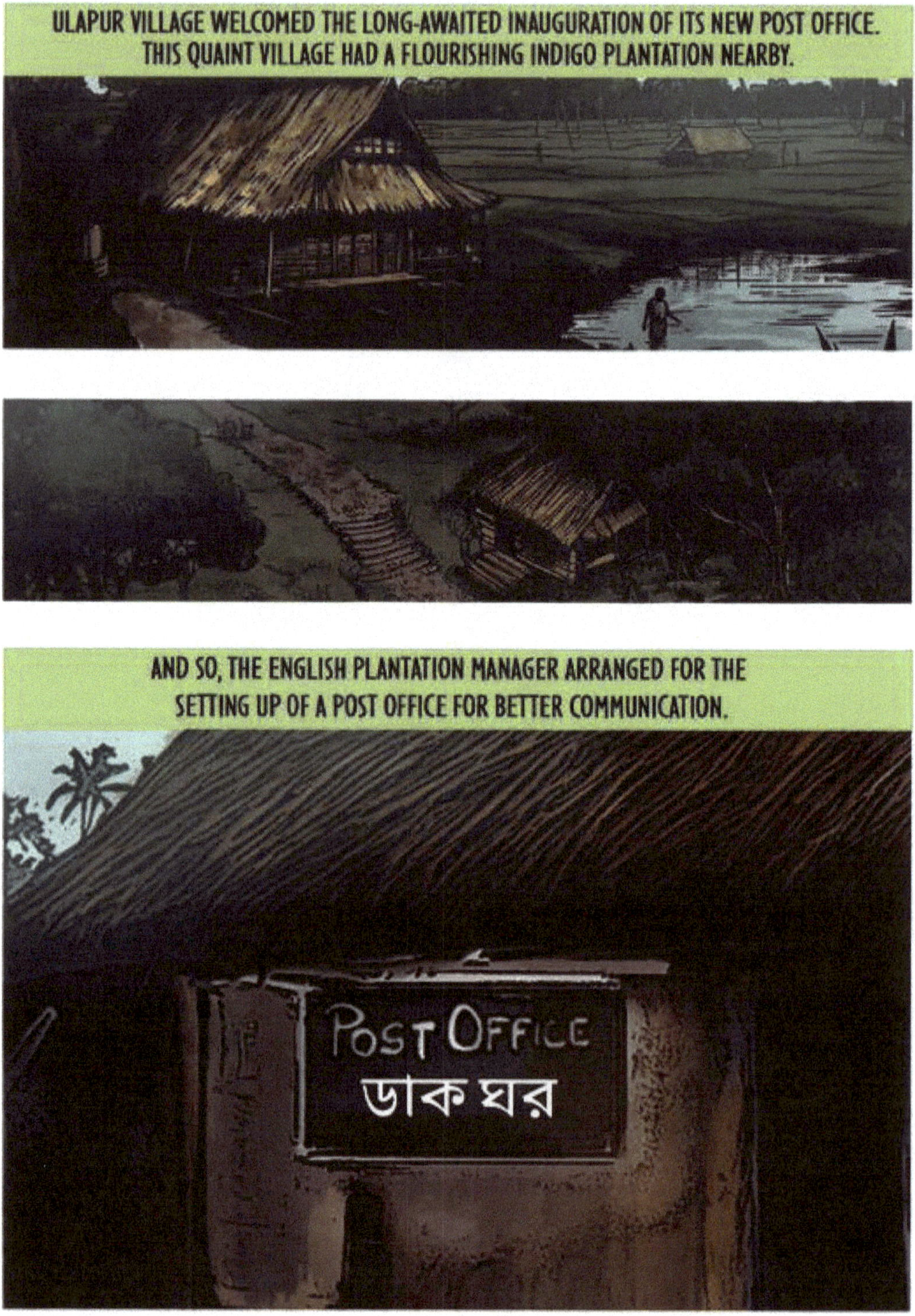
ULAPUR VILLAGE WELCOMED THE LONG-AWAITED INAUGURATION OF ITS NEW POST OFFICE. THIS QUAINT VILLAGE HAD A FLOURISHING INDIGO PLANTATION NEARBY.
AND SO, THE ENGLISH PLANTATION MANAGER ARRANGED FOR THE SETTING UP OF A POST OFFICE FOR BETTER COMMUNICATION.
POST OFFICE
ডাক ঘর

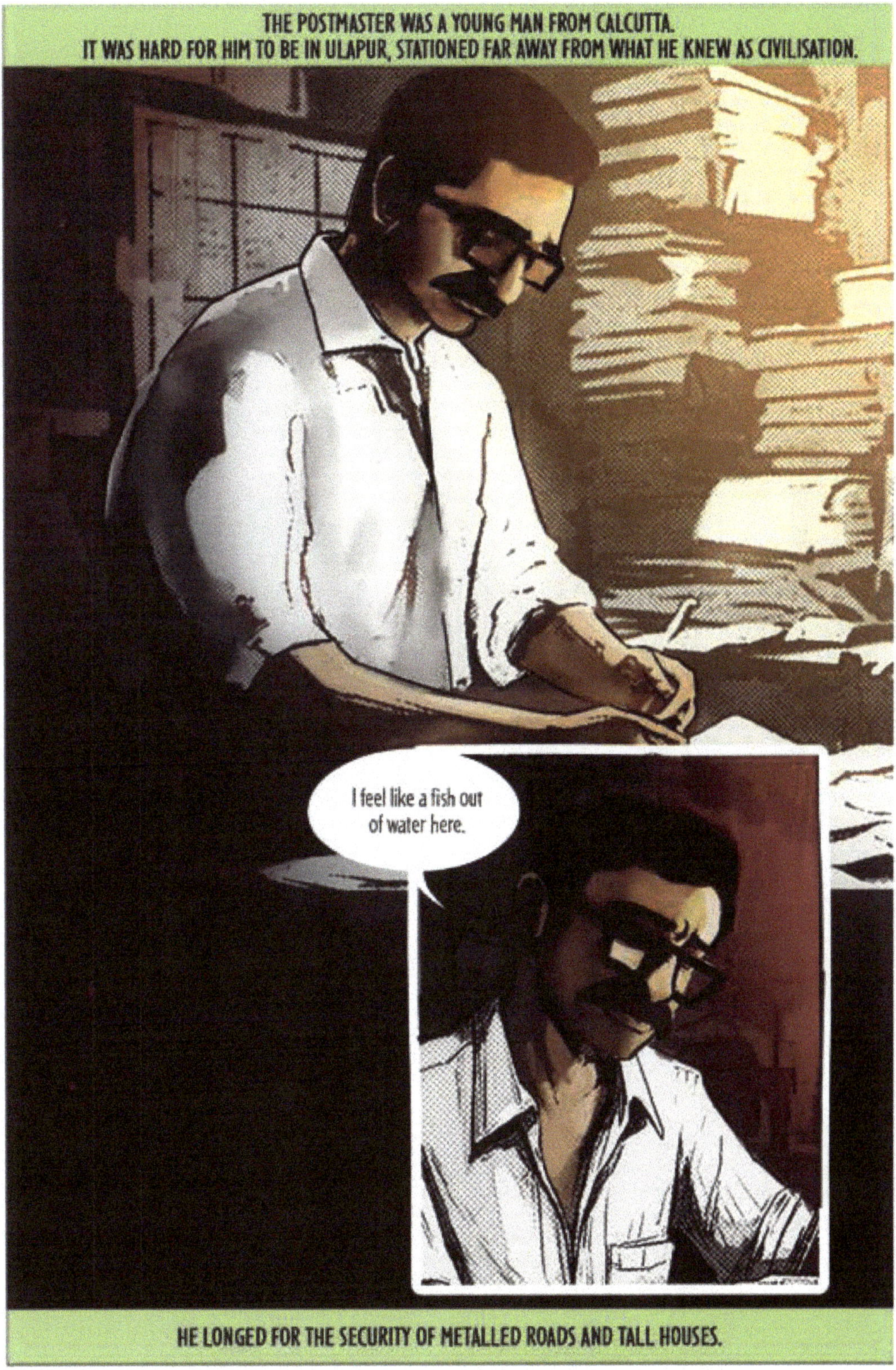
THE POSTMASTER WAS A YOUNG MAN FROM CALCUTTA.
IT WAS HARD FOR HIM TO BE IN ULAPUR, STATIONED FAR AWAY FROM WHAT HE KNEW AS CIVILISATION.
I feel like a fish out of water here.
HE LONGED FOR THE SECURITY OF METALLED ROADS AND TALL HOUSES.

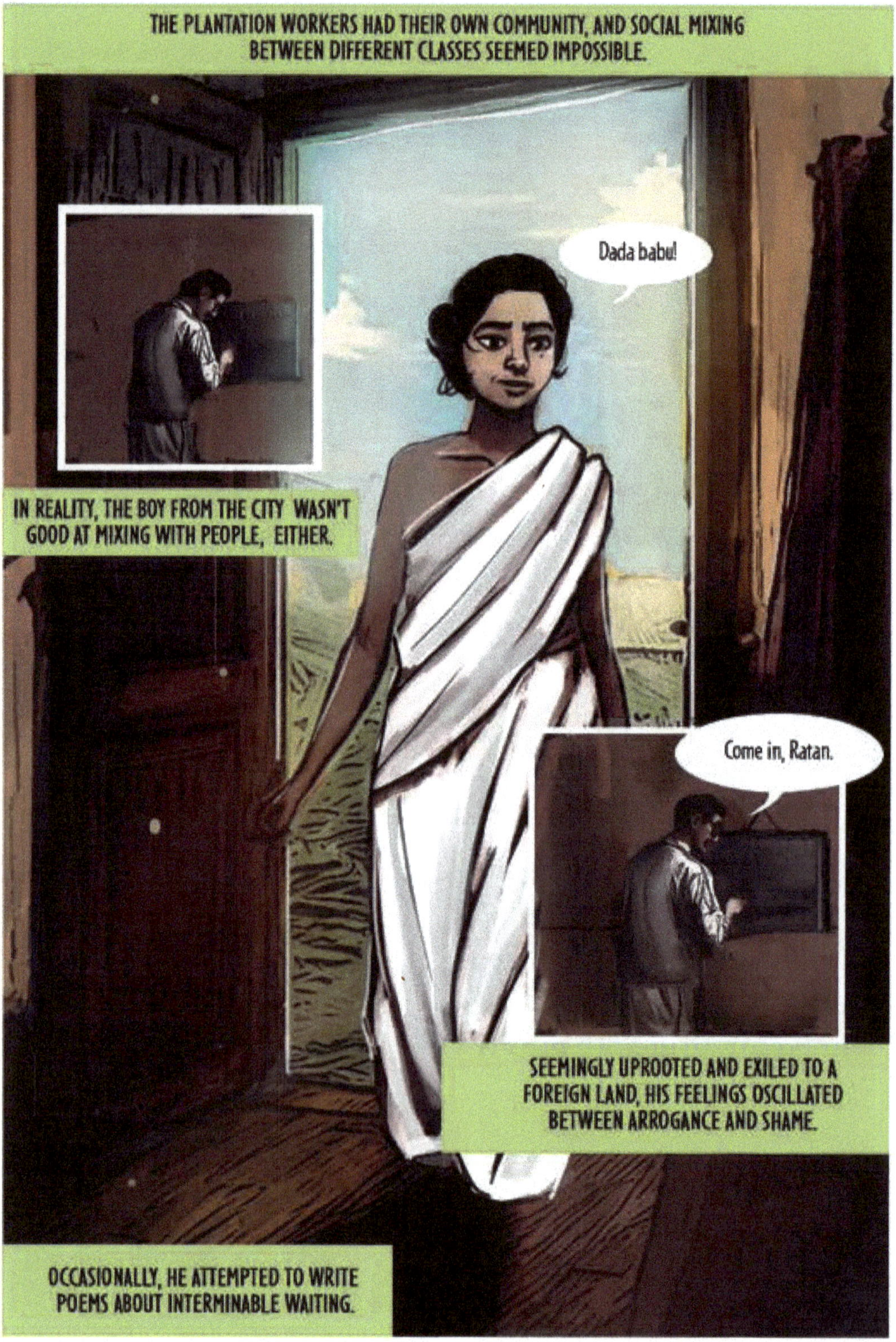
THE PLANTATION WORKERS HAD THEIR OWN COMMUNITY, AND SOCIAL MIXING BETWEEN DIFFERENT CLASSES SEEMED IMPOSSIBLE.
IN REALITY, THE BOY FROM THE CITY WASN'T GOOD AT MIXING WITH PEOPLE, EITHER.
Dada babu!
Come in, Ratan.
SEEMINGLY UPROOTED AND EXILED TO A FOREIGN LAND, HIS FEELINGS OSCILLATED BETWEEN ARROGANCE AND SHAME.
OCCASIONALLY, HE ATTEMPTED TO WRITE POEMS ABOUT INTERMINABLE WAITING.

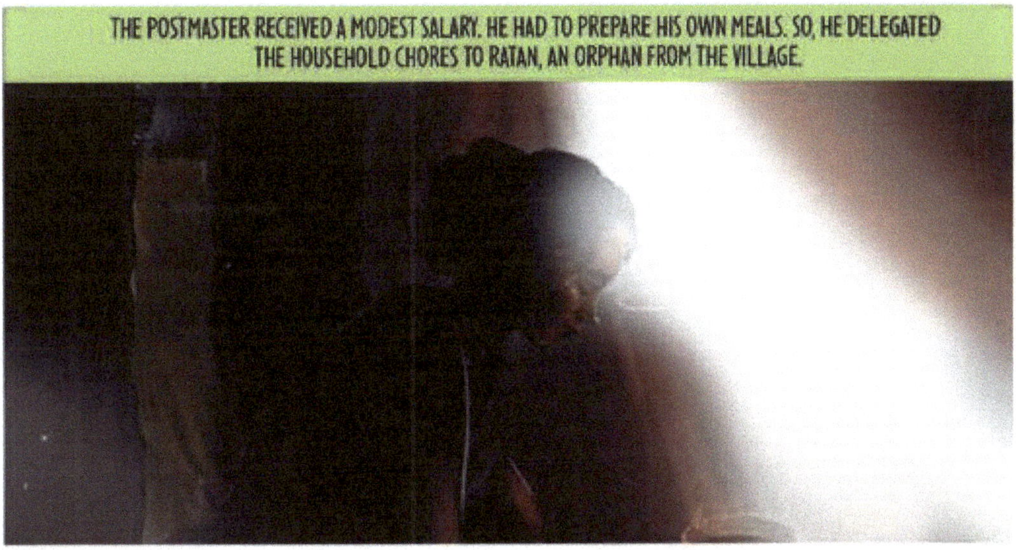
THE POSTMASTER RECEIVED A MODEST SALARY. HE HAD TO PREPARE HIS OWN MEALS. SO, HE DELEGATED THE HOUSEHOLD CHORES TO RATAN, AN ORPHAN FROM THE VILLAGE.

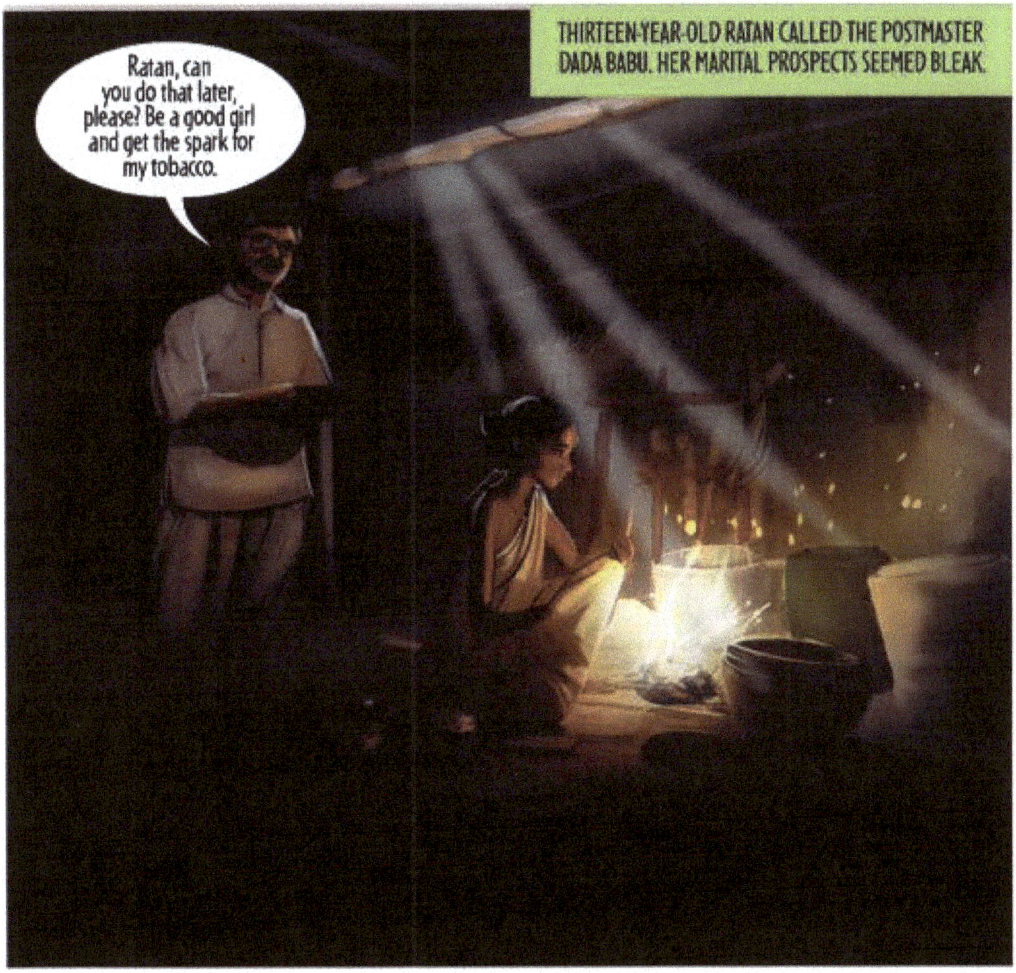
THIRTEEN-YEAR-OLD RATAN CALLED THE POSTMASTER DADA BABU. HER MARITAL PROSPECTS SEEMED BLEAK.
Ratan, can you do that later, please? Be a good girl and get the spark for my tobacco.

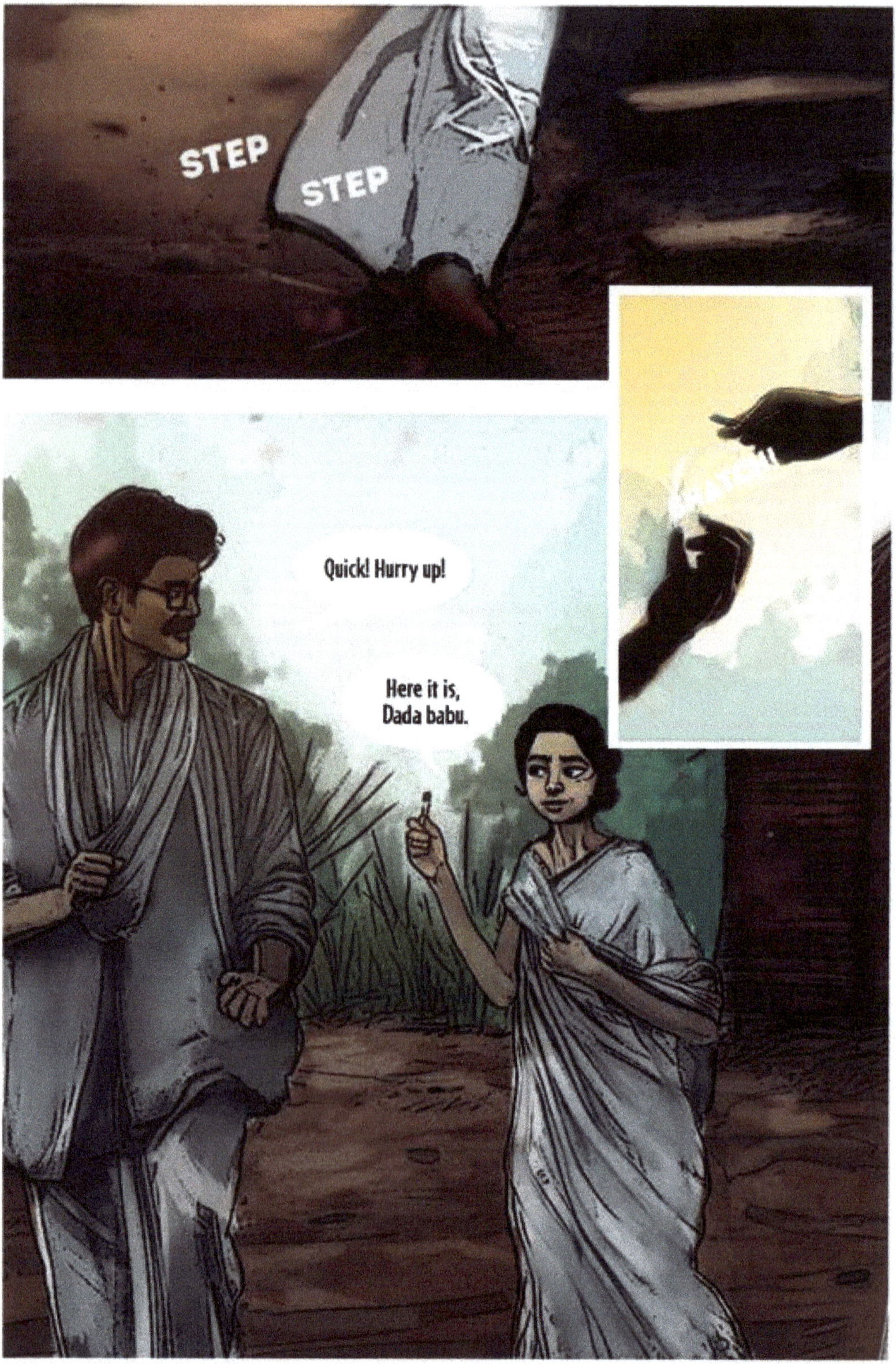
STEP
STEP
Quick! Hurry up!
Here it is, Dada babu.

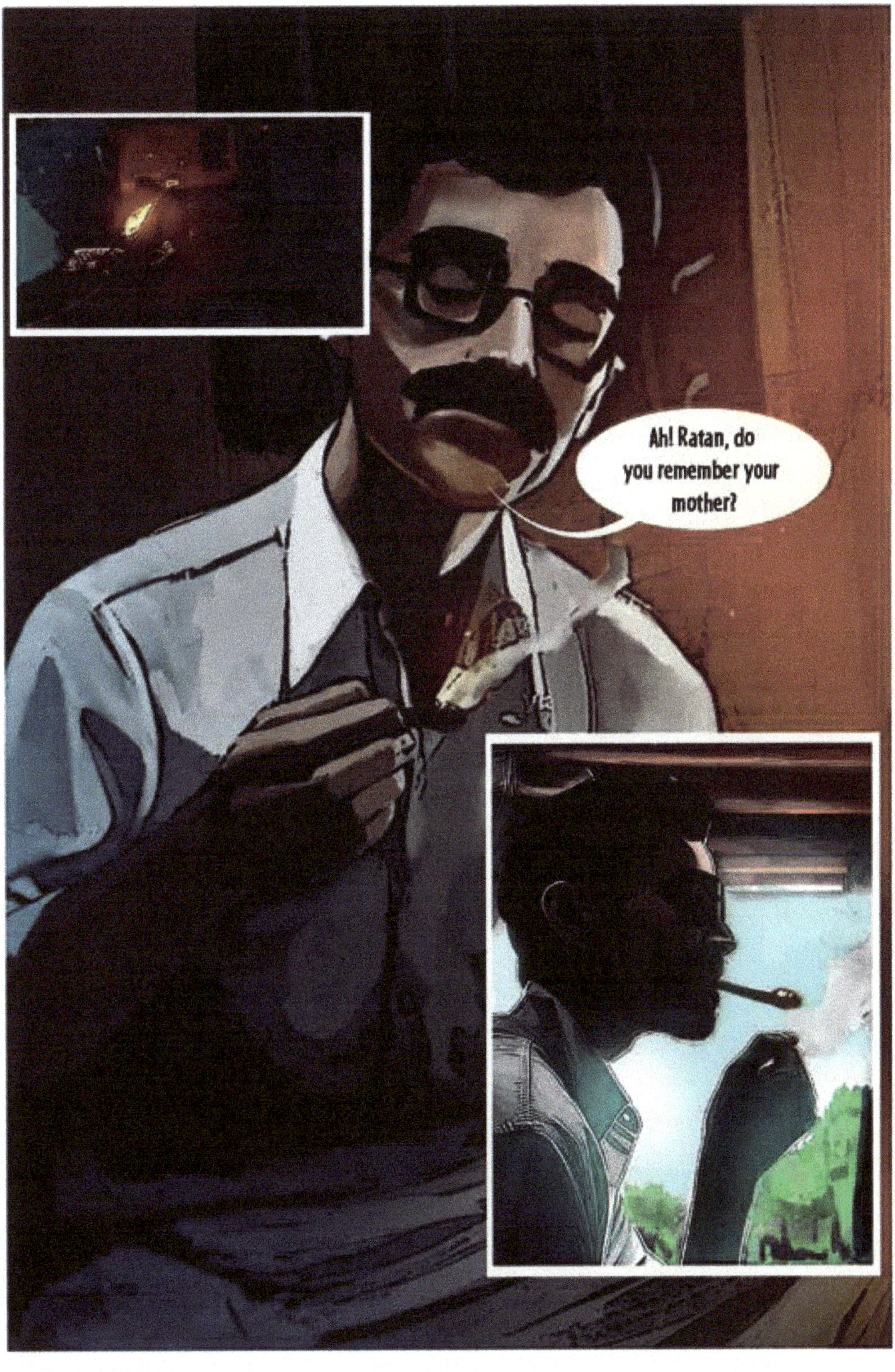
Ah! Ratan, do
you remember your
mother?

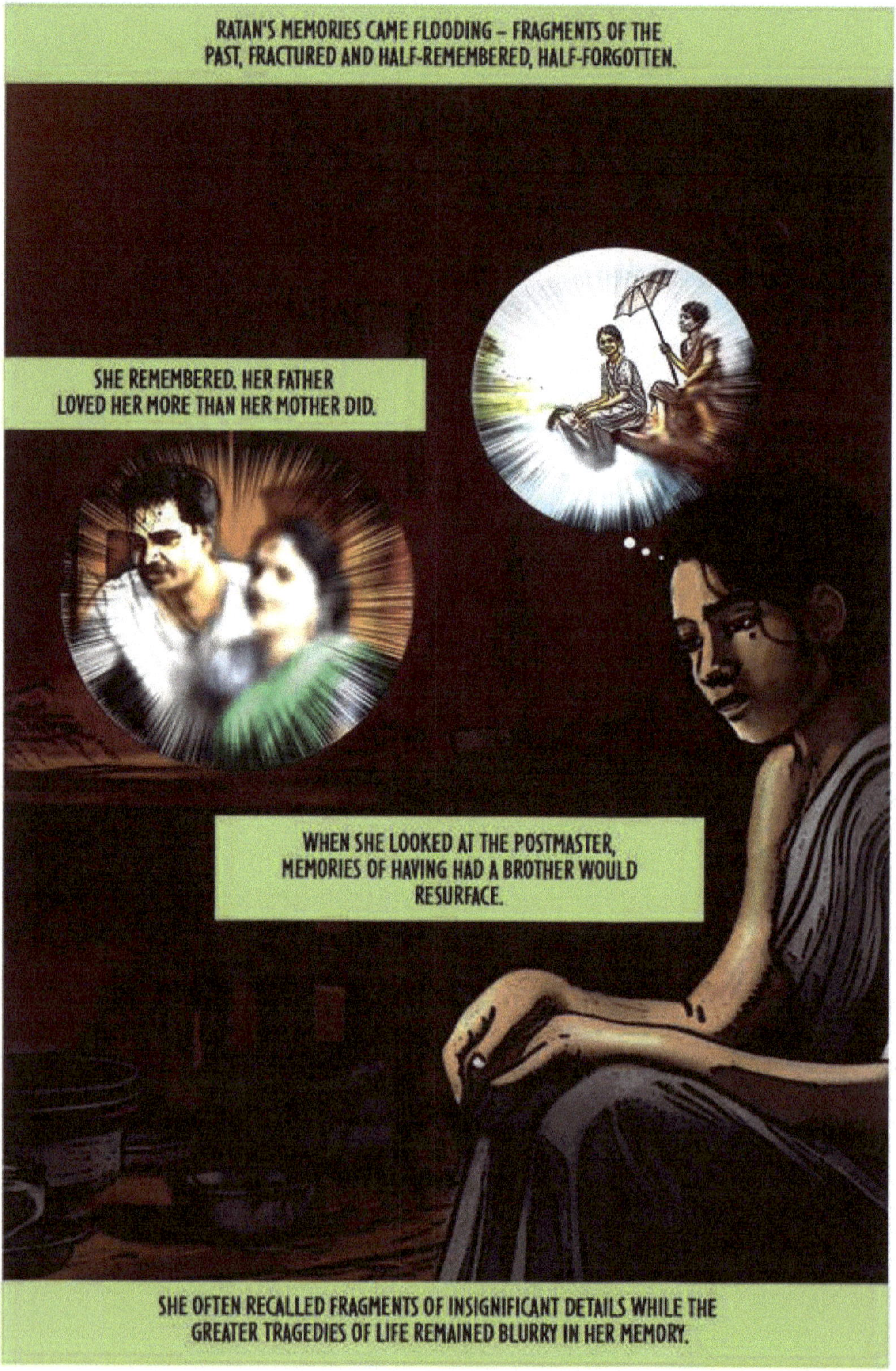
RATAN'S MEMORIES CAME FLOODING – FRAGMENTS OF THE PAST, FRACTURED AND HALF-REMEMBERED, HALF-FORGOTTEN.
SHE REMEMBERED. HER FATHER LOVED HER MORE THAN HER MOTHER DID.
WHEN SHE LOOKED AT THE POSTMASTER, MEMORIES OF HAVING HAD A BROTHER WOULD RESURFACE.
SHE OFTEN RECALLED FRAGMENTS OF INSIGNIFICANT DETAILS WHILE THE GREATER TRAGEDIES OF LIFE REMAINED BLURRY IN HER MEMORY.

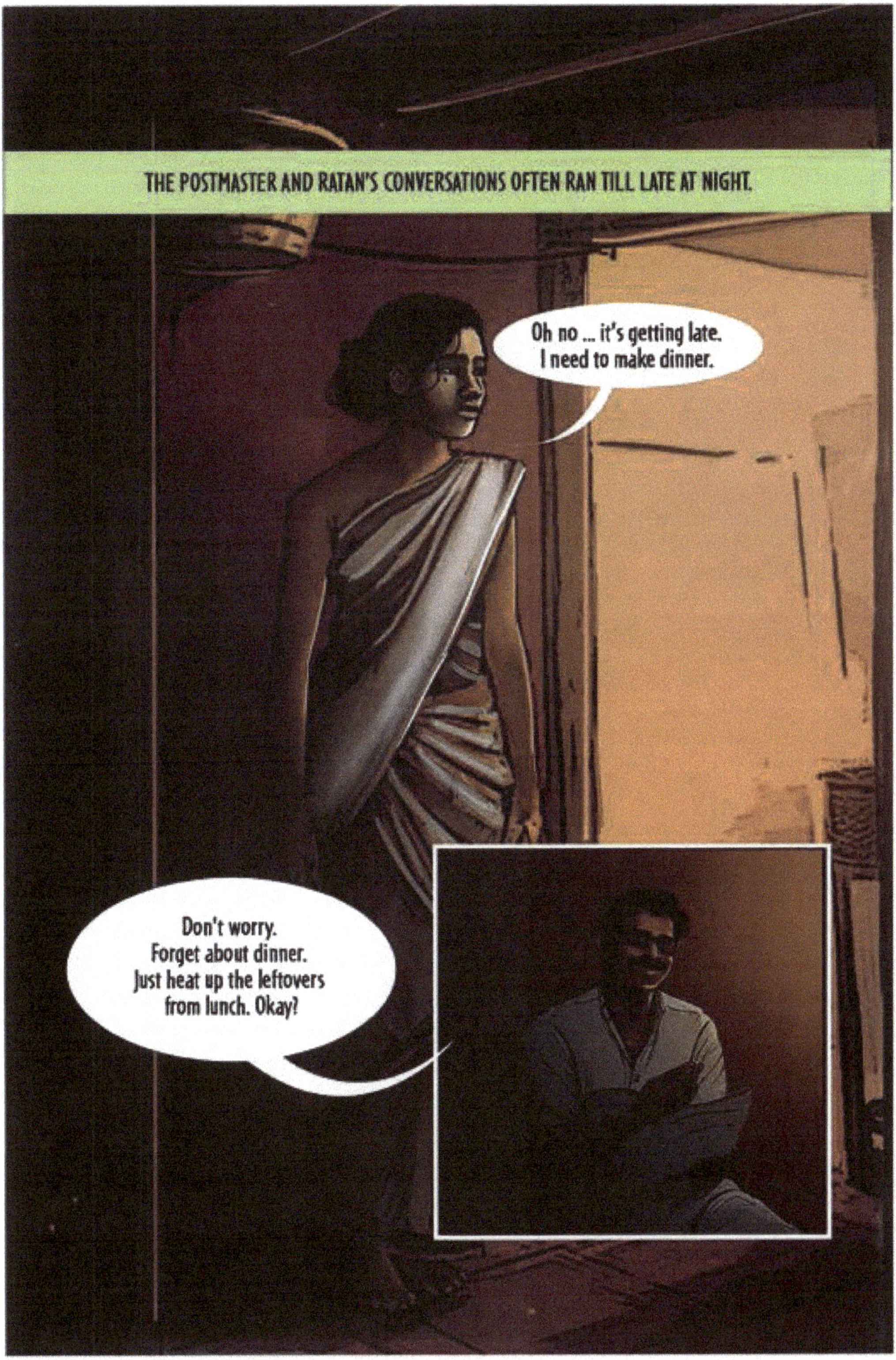
THE POSTMASTER AND RATAN'S CONVERSATIONS OFTEN RAN TILL LATE AT NIGHT.
Oh no ... it's getting late. I need to make dinner.
Don't worry. Forget about dinner. Just heat up the leftovers from lunch. Okay?

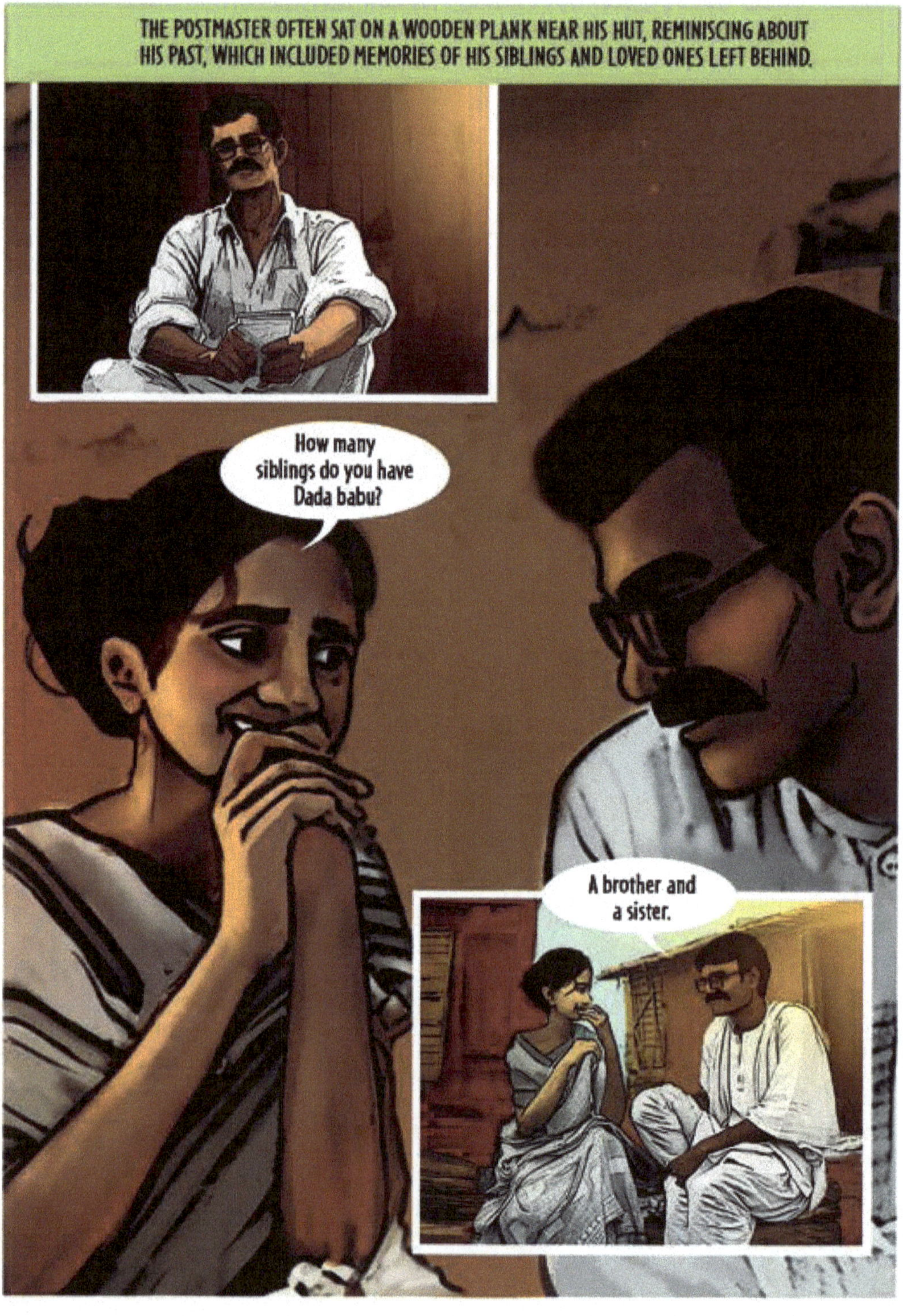
THE POSTMASTER OFTEN SAT ON A WOODEN PLANK NEAR HIS HUT, REMINISCING ABOUT HIS PAST, WHICH INCLUDED MEMORIES OF HIS SIBLINGS AND LOVED ONES LEFT BEHIND.
How many siblings do you have Dada babu?
A brother and a sister.

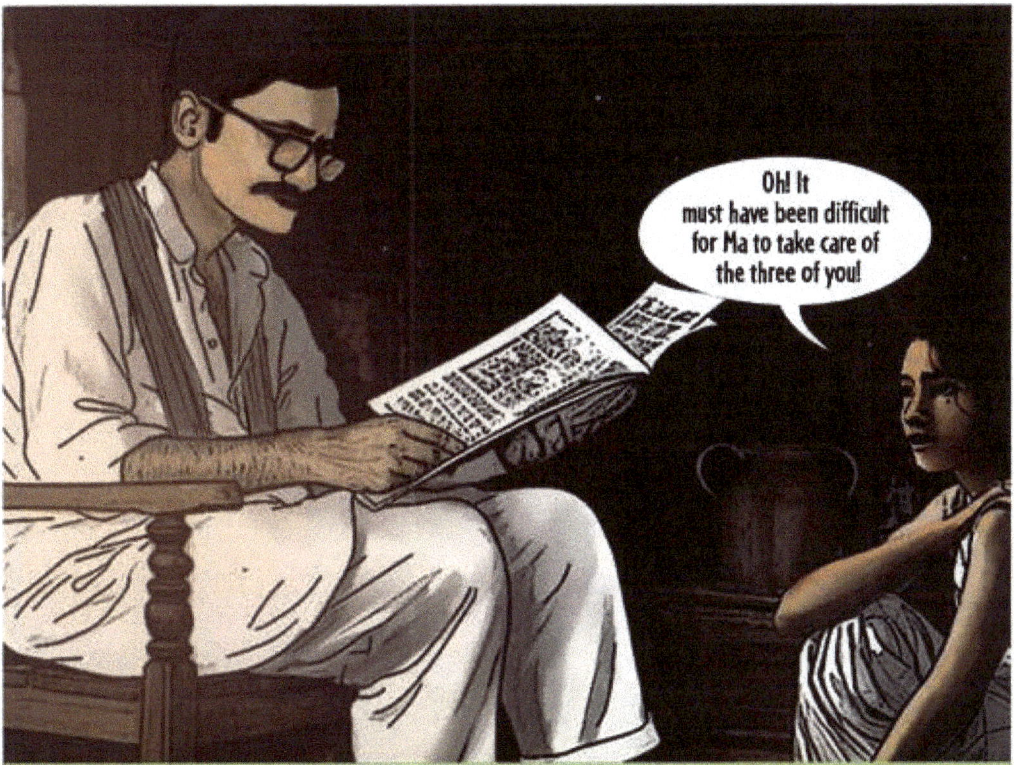
Oh! It must have been difficult for Ma to take care of the three of you!

OVER TIME, RATAN STARTED ADDRESSING THE CHARACTERS IN THE POSTMASTER'S TALES BY THEIR RELATIONSHIP TO HIM, TRANSFORMING PERSONAL HISTORY INTO A SHARED MEMORY.

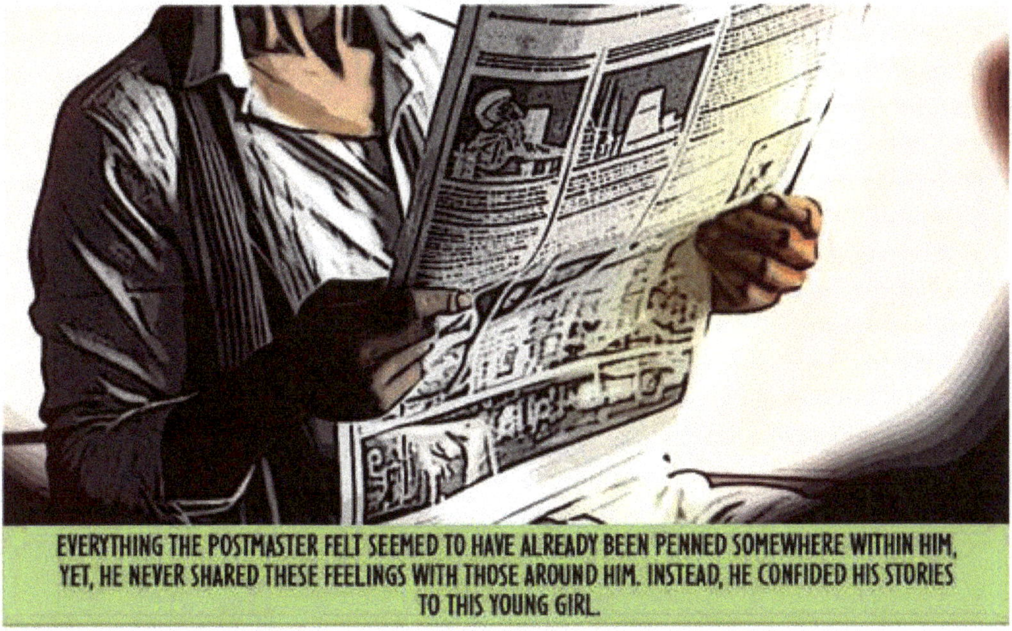

EVERYTHING THE POSTMASTER FELT SEEMED TO HAVE ALREADY BEEN PENNED SOMEWHERE WITHIN HIM, YET, HE NEVER SHARED THESE FEELINGS WITH THOSE AROUND HIM. INSTEAD, HE CONFIDED HIS STORIES TO THIS YOUNG GIRL.

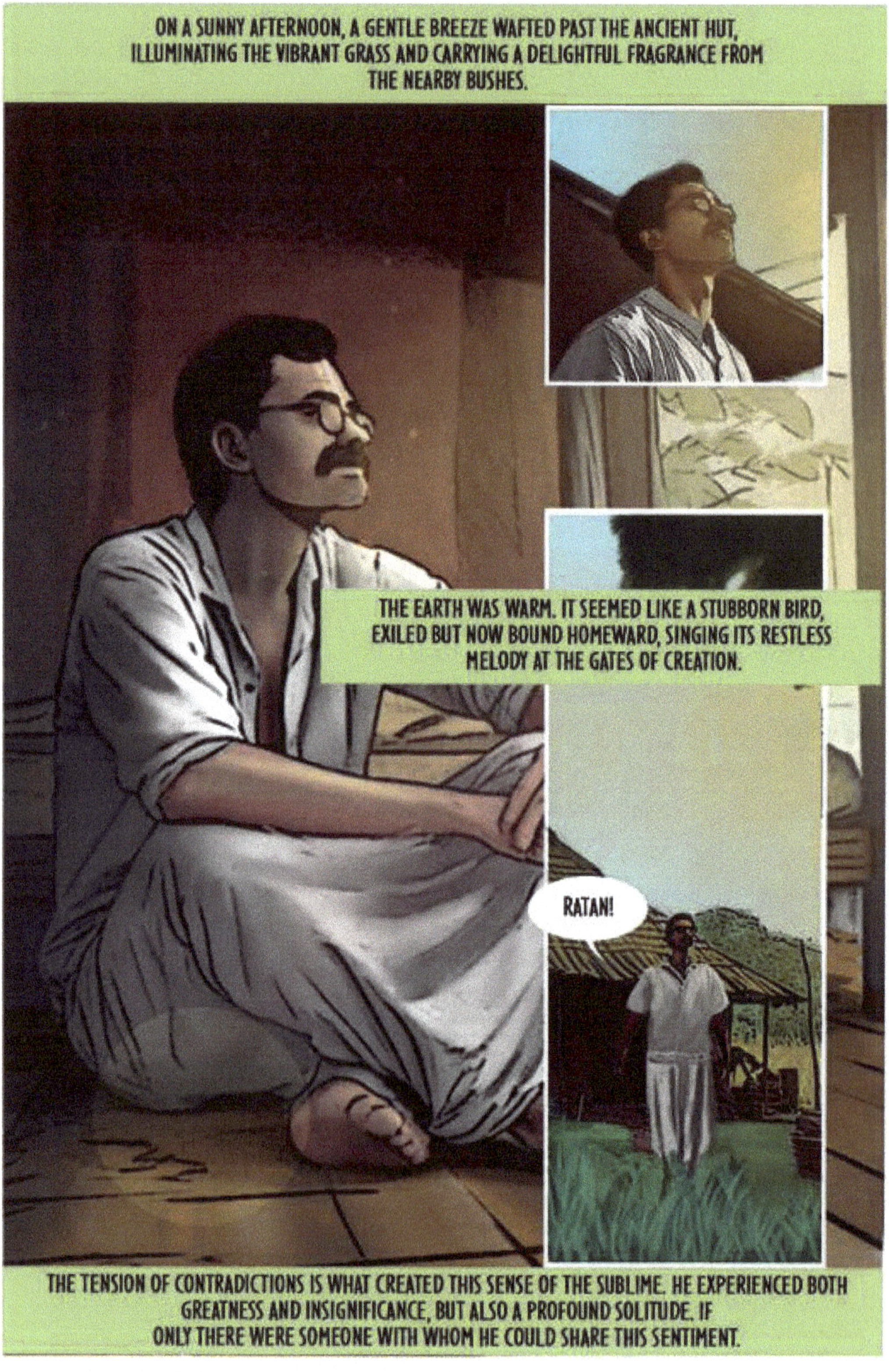
ON A SUNNY AFTERNOON, A GENTLE BREEZE WAFTED PAST THE ANCIENT HUT, ILLUMINATING THE VIBRANT GRASS AND CARRYING A DELIGHTFUL FRAGRANCE FROM THE NEARBY BUSHES.
THE EARTH WAS WARM. IT SEEMED LIKE A STUBBORN BIRD, EXILED BUT NOW BOUND HOMEWARD, SINGING ITS RESTLESS MELODY AT THE GATES OF CREATION.
RATAN!
THE TENSION OF CONTRADICTIONS IS WHAT CREATED THIS SENSE OF THE SUBLIME. HE EXPERIENCED BOTH GREATNESS AND INSIGNIFICANCE, BUT ALSO A PROFOUND SOLITUDE. IF ONLY THERE WERE SOMEONE WITH WHOM HE COULD SHARE THIS SENTIMENT.

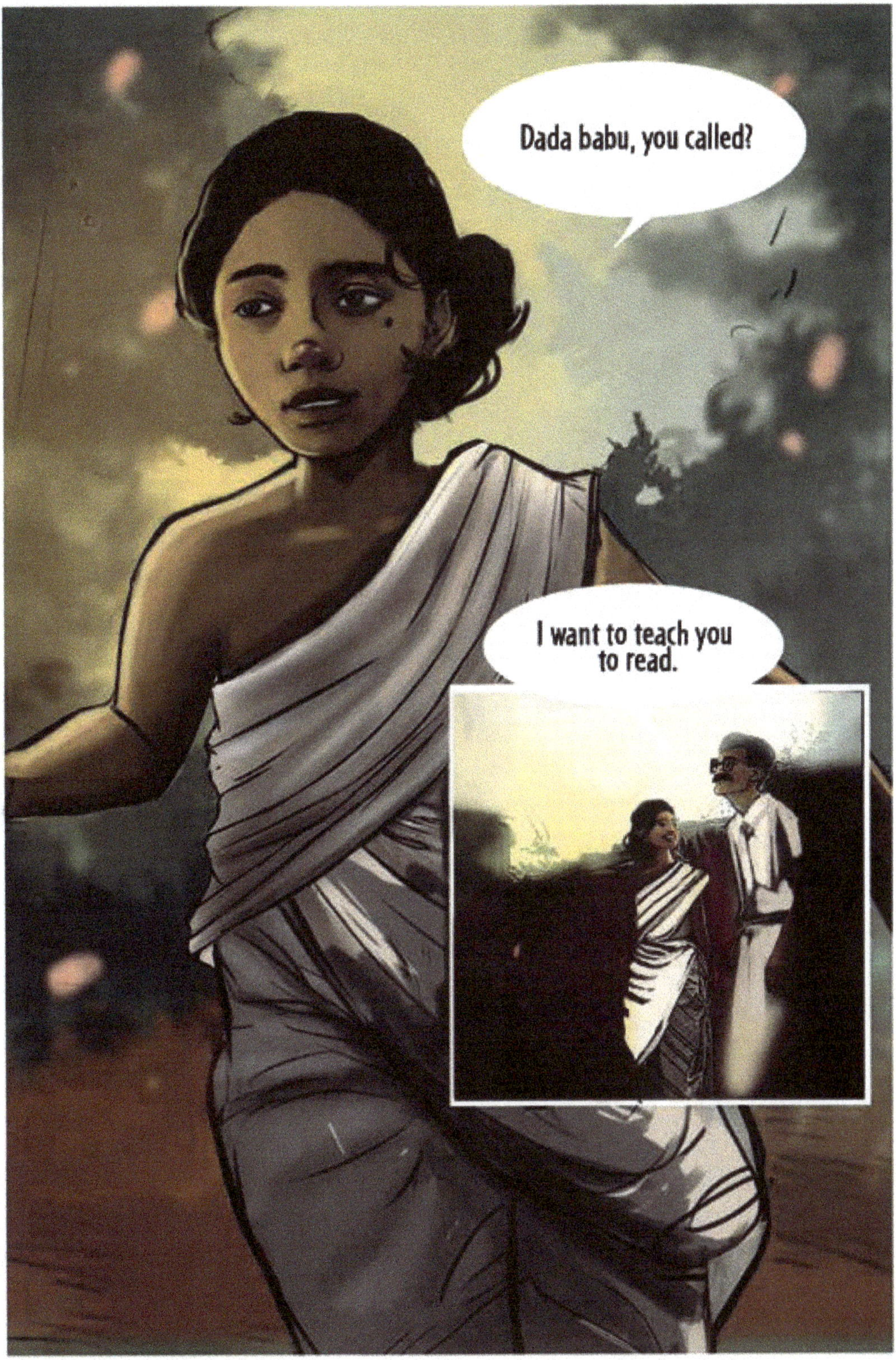
Dada babu, you called?
I want to teach you to read.

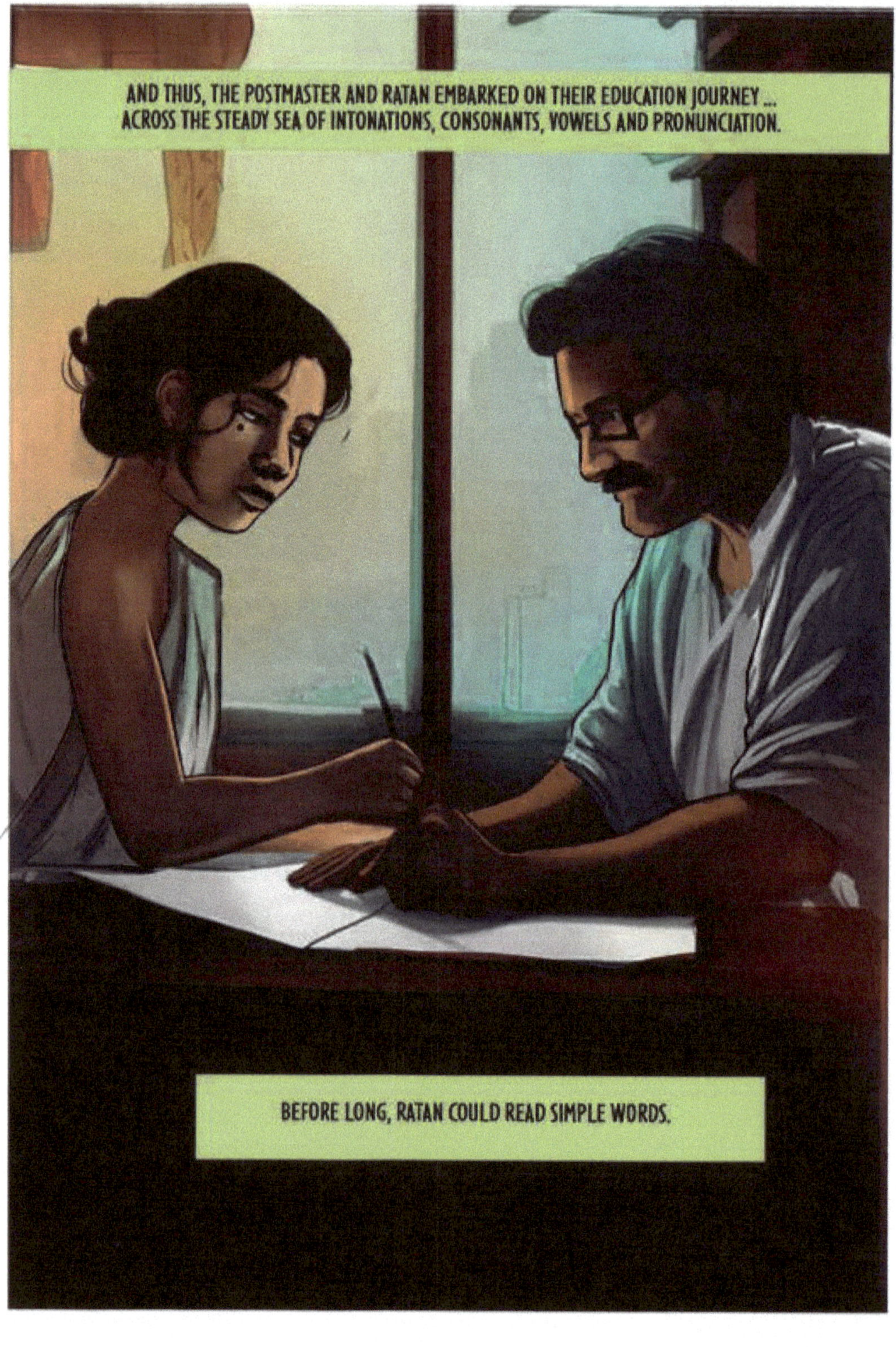
AND THUS, THE POSTMASTER AND RATAN EMBARKED ON THEIR EDUCATION JOURNEY ...
ACROSS THE STEADY SEA OF INTONATIONS, CONSONANTS, VOWELS AND PRONUNCIATION.
BEFORE LONG, RATAN COULD READ SIMPLE WORDS.

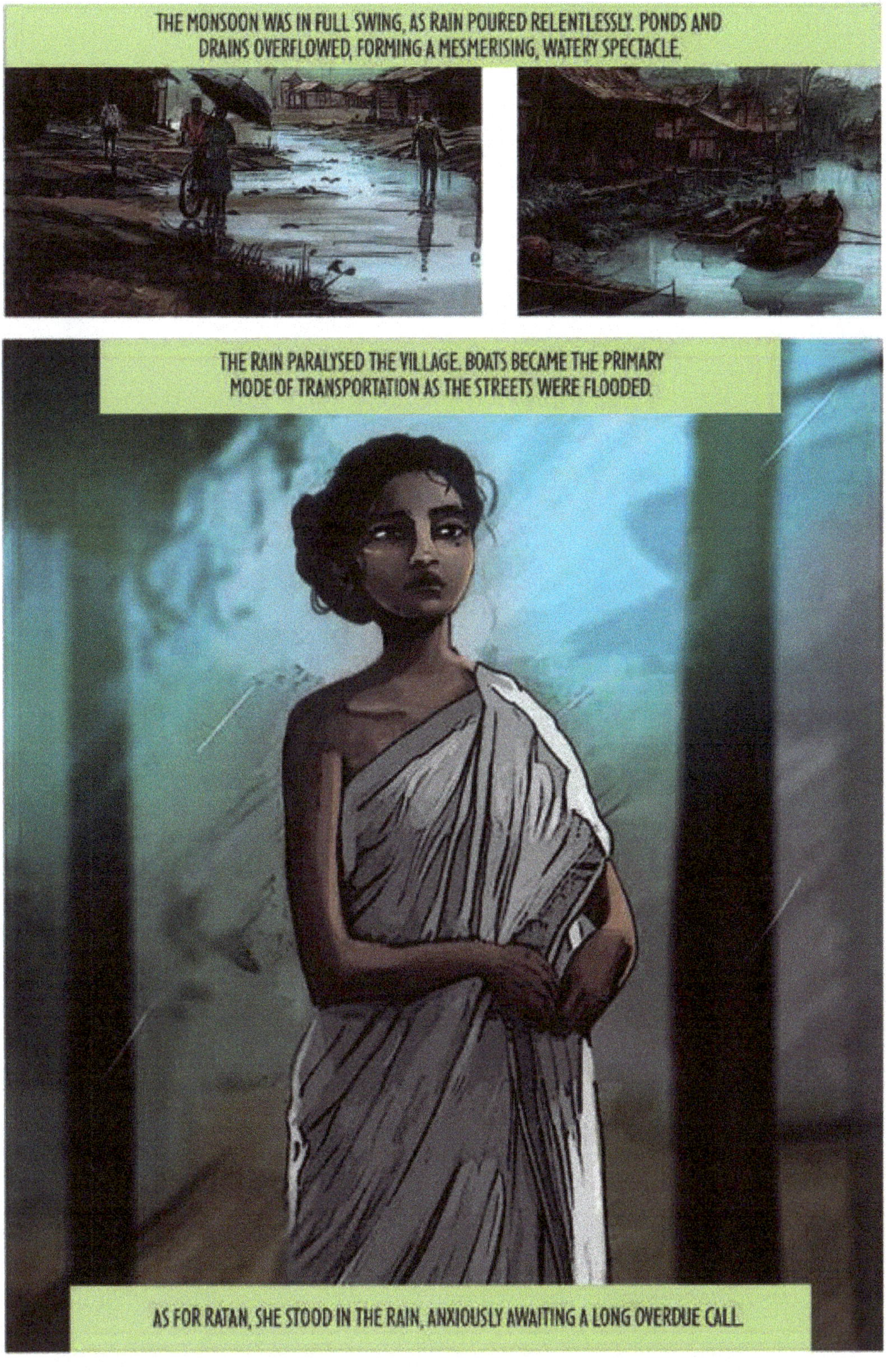
THE MONSOON WAS IN FULL SWING, AS RAIN POURED RELENTLESSLY. PONDS AND DRAINS OVERFLOWED, FORMING A MESMERISING, WATERY SPECTACLE.
THE RAIN PARALYSED THE VILLAGE. BOATS BECAME THE PRIMARY MODE OF TRANSPORTATION AS THE STREETS WERE FLOODED.
AS FOR RATAN, SHE STOOD IN THE RAIN, ANXIOUSLY AWAITING A LONG OVERDUE CALL.

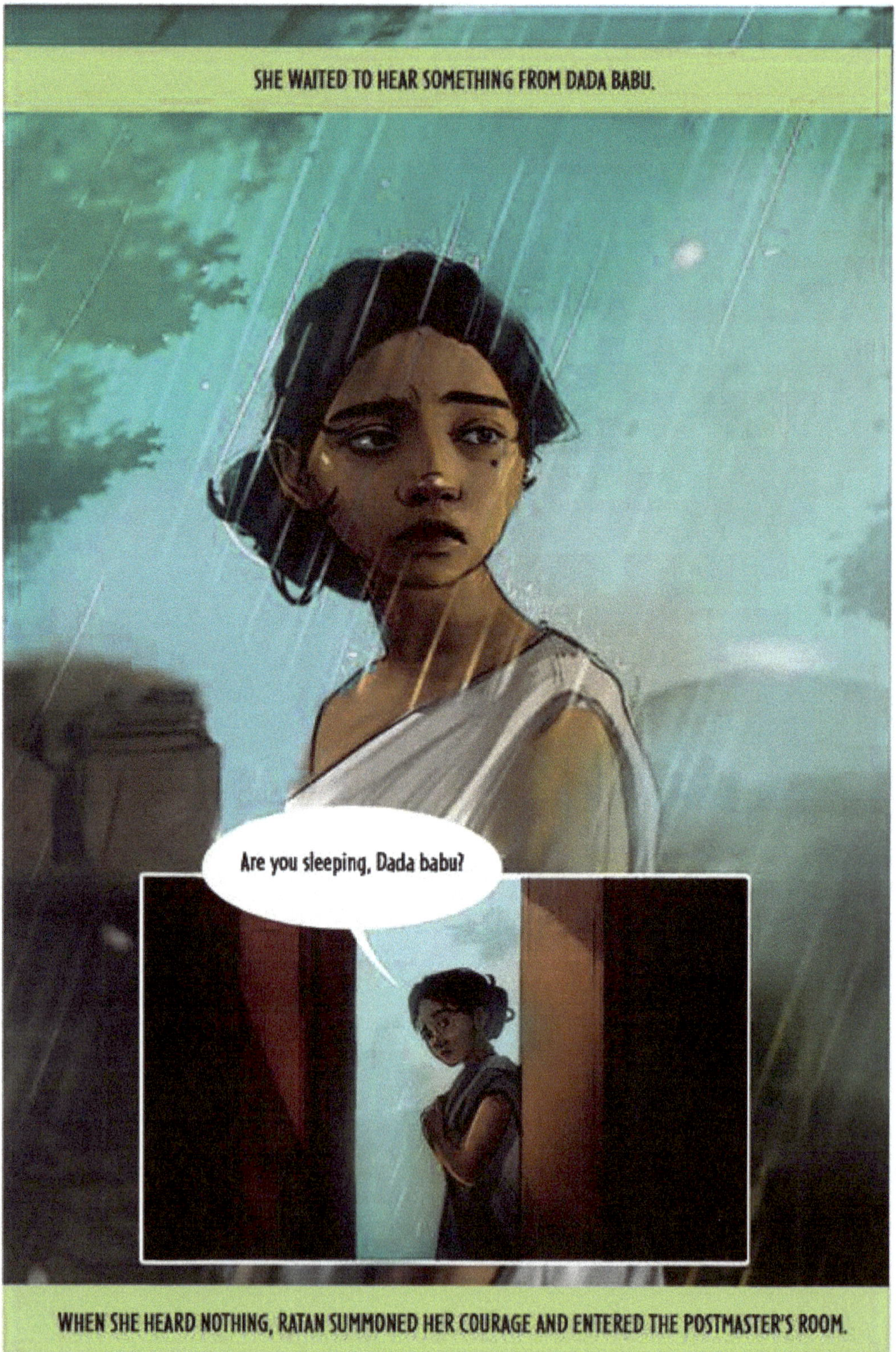
SHE WAITED TO HEAR SOMETHING FROM DADA BABU.
Are you sleeping, Dada babu?
WHEN SHE HEARD NOTHING, RATAN SUMMONED HER COURAGE AND ENTERED THE POSTMASTER'S ROOM.

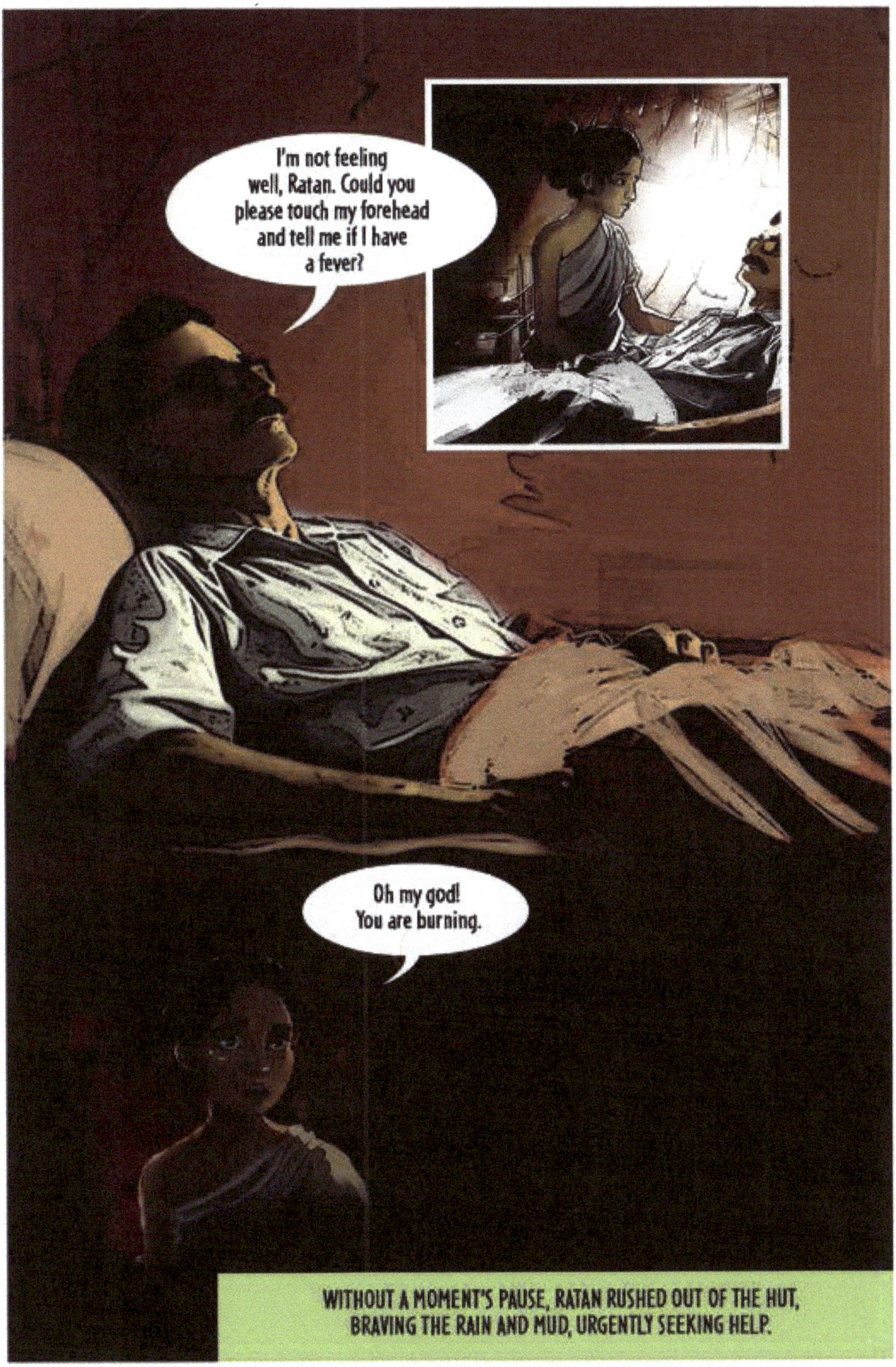
I'm not feeling well, Ratan. Could you please touch my forehead and tell me if I have a fever?
Oh my god! You are burning.
WITHOUT A MOMENT'S PAUSE, RATAN RUSHED OUT OF THE HUT, BRAVING THE RAIN AND MUD, URGENTLY SEEKING HELP.

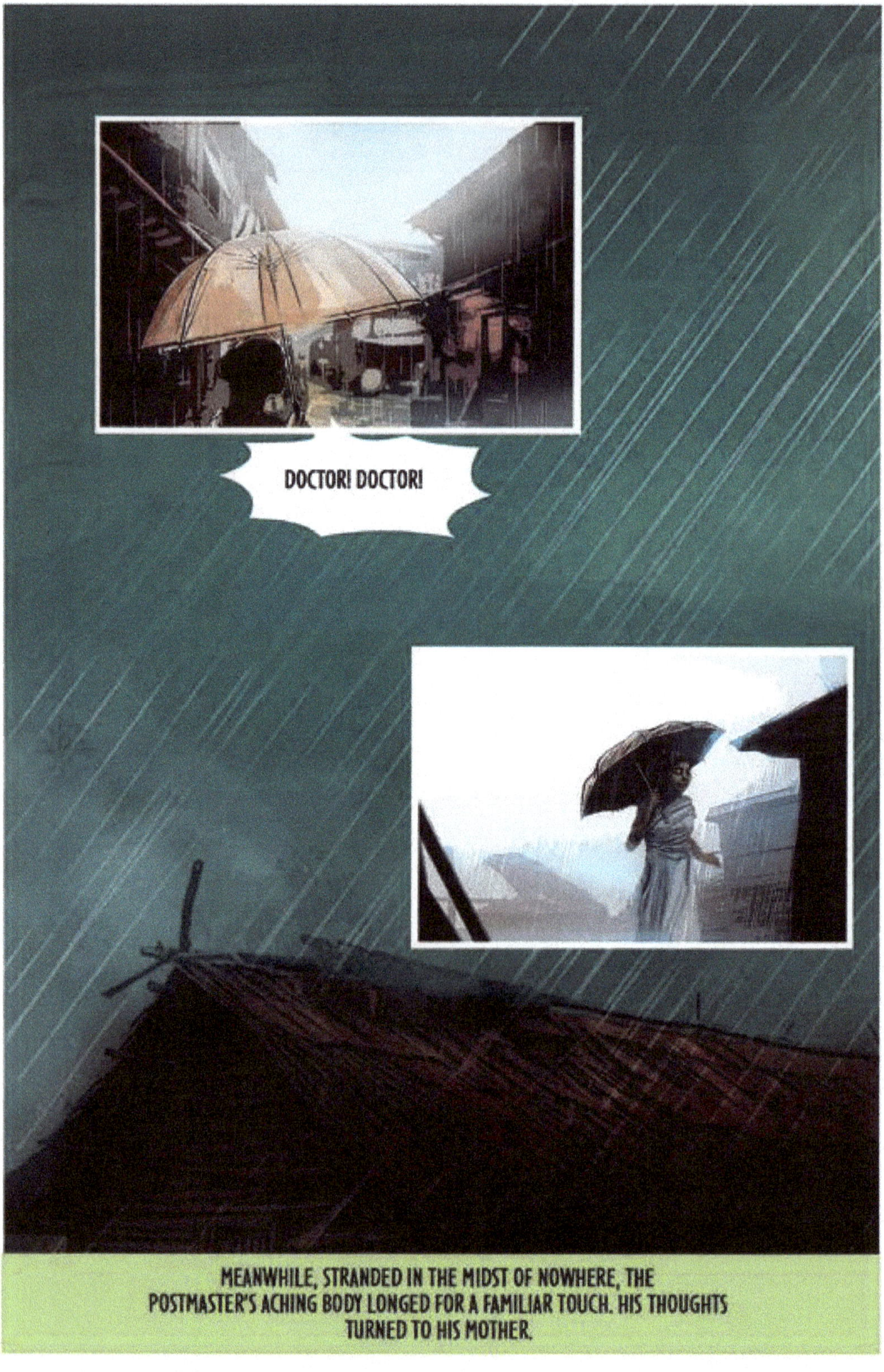
DOCTOR! DOCTOR!
MEANWHILE, STRANDED IN THE MIDST OF NOWHERE, THE POSTMASTER'S ACHING BODY LONGED FOR A FAMILIAR TOUCH. HIS THOUGHTS TURNED TO HIS MOTHER.

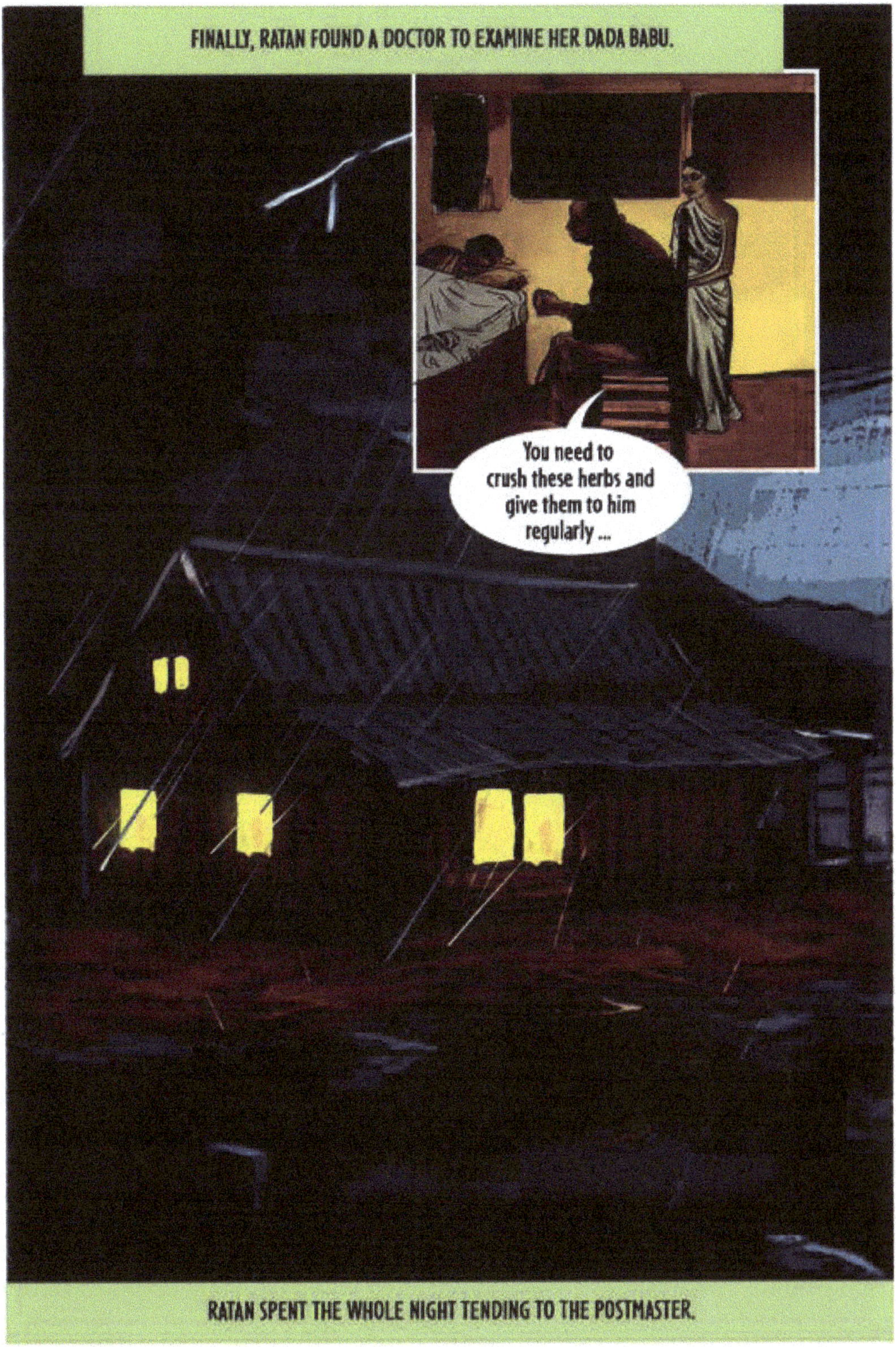
FINALLY, RATAN FOUND A DOCTOR TO EXAMINE HER DADA BABU.
You need to crush these herbs and give them to him regularly ...
RATAN SPENT THE WHOLE NIGHT TENDING TO THE POSTMASTER.

SHE STAYED UP ALL NIGHT, CRUSHING THE HERBS AND PREPARING REMEDIES TO ALLEVIATE THE POSTMASTER'S DISCOMFORT.

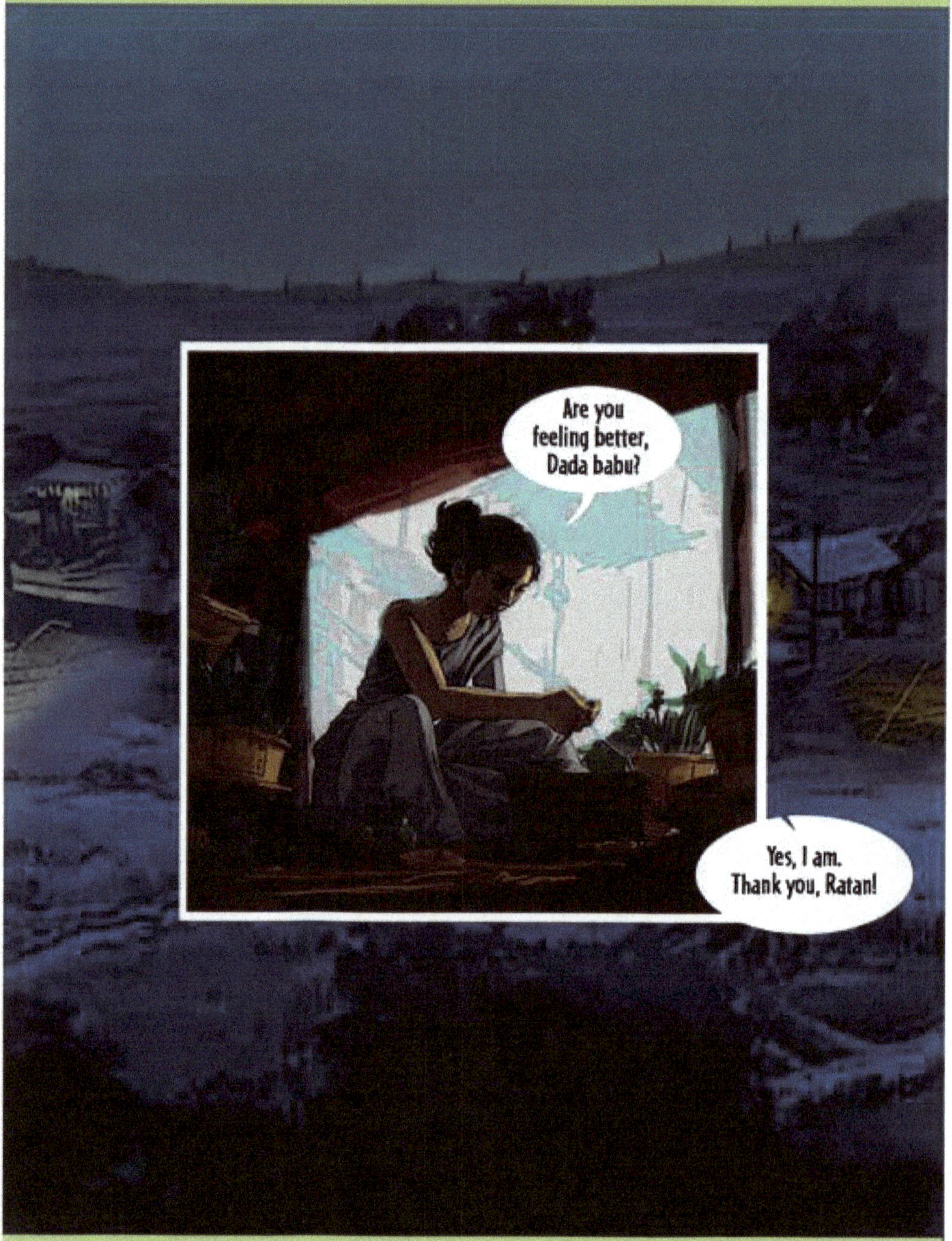

Are you feeling better, Dada babu?
Yes, I am. Thank you, Ratan!

IT TOOK WEEKS, BUT THE POSTMASTER GRADUALLY RECOVERED FROM HIS ILLNESS UNDER RATAN'S DILIGENT CARE. HIS STRENGTH RETURNED, AND HE FELT A RENEWED SENSE OF VITALITY.

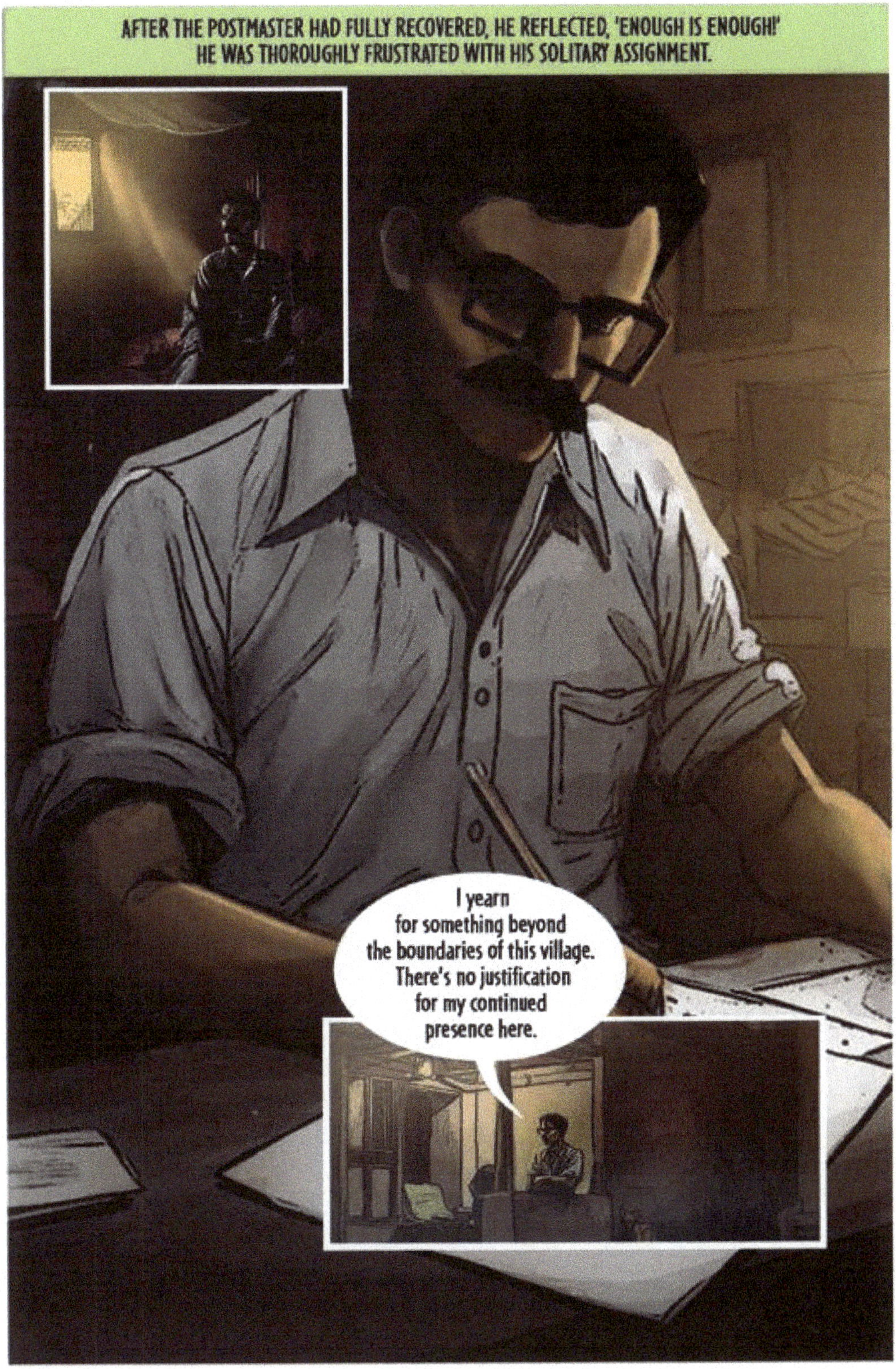
AFTER THE POSTMASTER HAD FULLY RECOVERED, HE REFLECTED, 'ENOUGH IS ENOUGH!' HE WAS THOROUGHLY FRUSTRATED WITH HIS SOLITARY ASSIGNMENT.
I yearn for something beyond the boundaries of this village. There's no justification for my continued presence here.

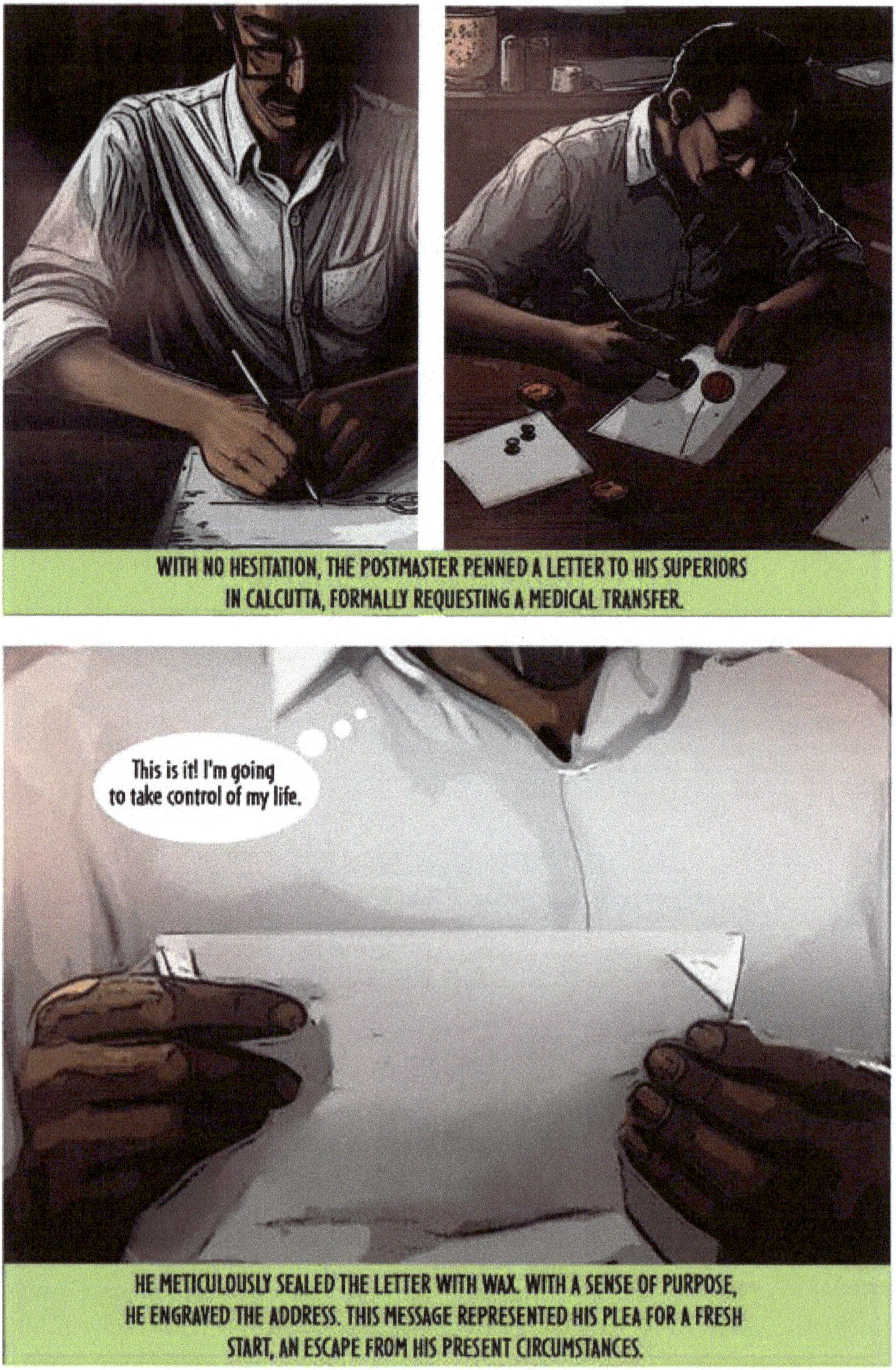
WITH NO HESITATION, THE POSTMASTER PENNED A LETTER TO HIS SUPERIORS IN CALCUTTA, FORMALLY REQUESTING A MEDICAL TRANSFER.
This is it! I'm going to take control of my life.
HE METICULOUSLY SEALED THE LETTER WITH WAX. WITH A SENSE OF PURPOSE, HE ENGRAVED THE ADDRESS. THIS MESSAGE REPRESENTED HIS PLEA FOR A FRESH START, AN ESCAPE FROM HIS PRESENT CIRCUMSTANCES.

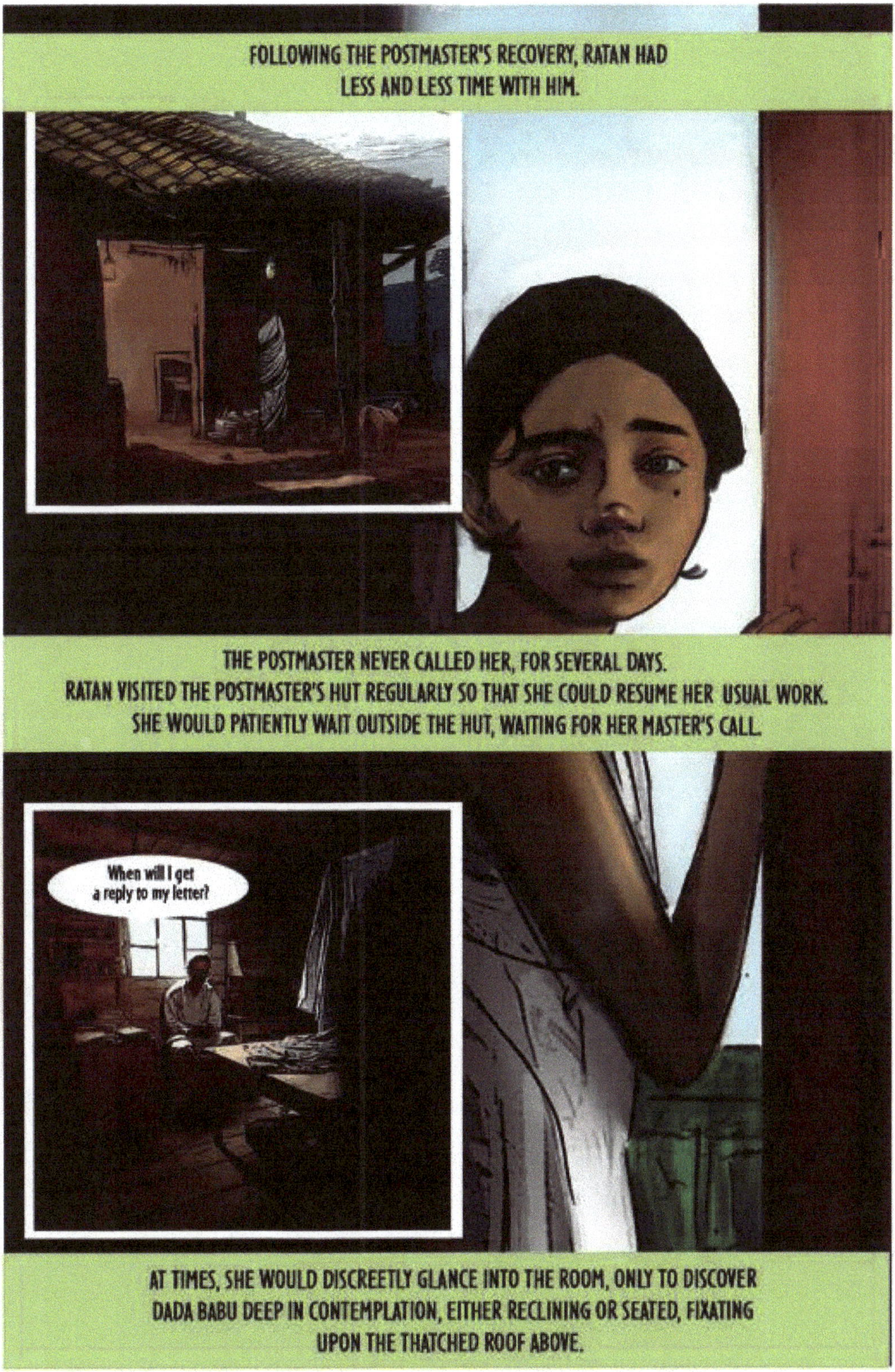
FOLLOWING THE POSTMASTER'S RECOVERY, RATAN HAD LESS AND LESS TIME WITH HIM.
THE POSTMASTER NEVER CALLED HER, FOR SEVERAL DAYS. RATAN VISITED THE POSTMASTER'S HUT REGULARLY SO THAT SHE COULD RESUME HER USUAL WORK. SHE WOULD PATIENTLY WAIT OUTSIDE THE HUT, WAITING FOR HER MASTER'S CALL.
When will I get a reply to my letter?
AT TIMES, SHE WOULD DISCREETLY GLANCE INTO THE ROOM, ONLY TO DISCOVER DADA BABU DEEP IN CONTEMPLATION, EITHER RECLINING OR SEATED, FIXATING UPON THE THATCHED ROOF ABOVE.

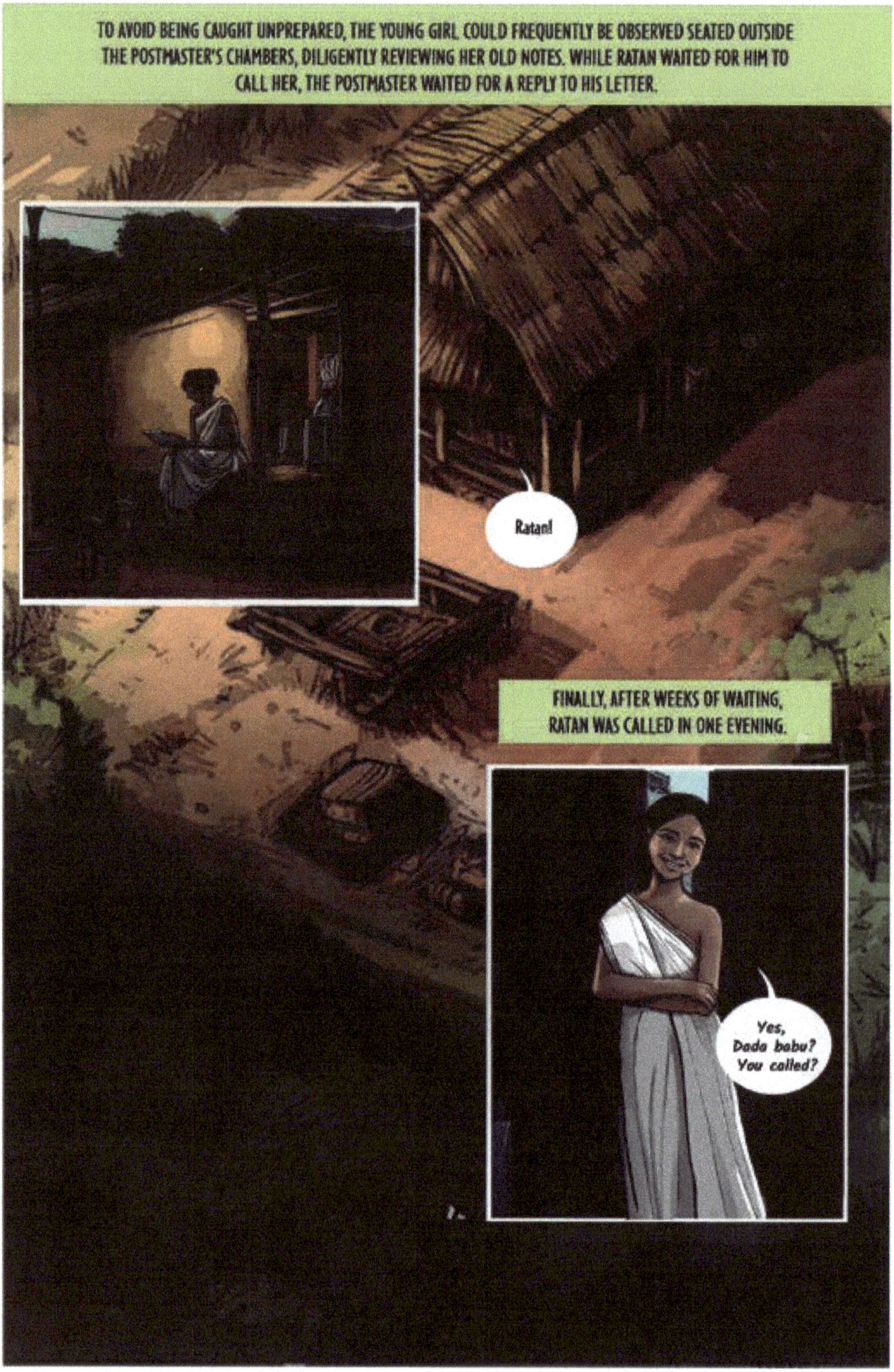
TO AVOID BEING CAUGHT UNPREPARED, THE YOUNG GIRL COULD FREQUENTLY BE OBSERVED SEATED OUTSIDE THE POSTMASTER'S CHAMBERS, DILIGENTLY REVIEWING HER OLD NOTES. WHILE RATAN WAITED FOR HIM TO CALL HER, THE POSTMASTER WAITED FOR A REPLY TO HIS LETTER.
Ratan!
FINALLY, AFTER WEEKS OF WAITING, RATAN WAS CALLED IN ONE EVENING.
Yes, Dada babu? You called?

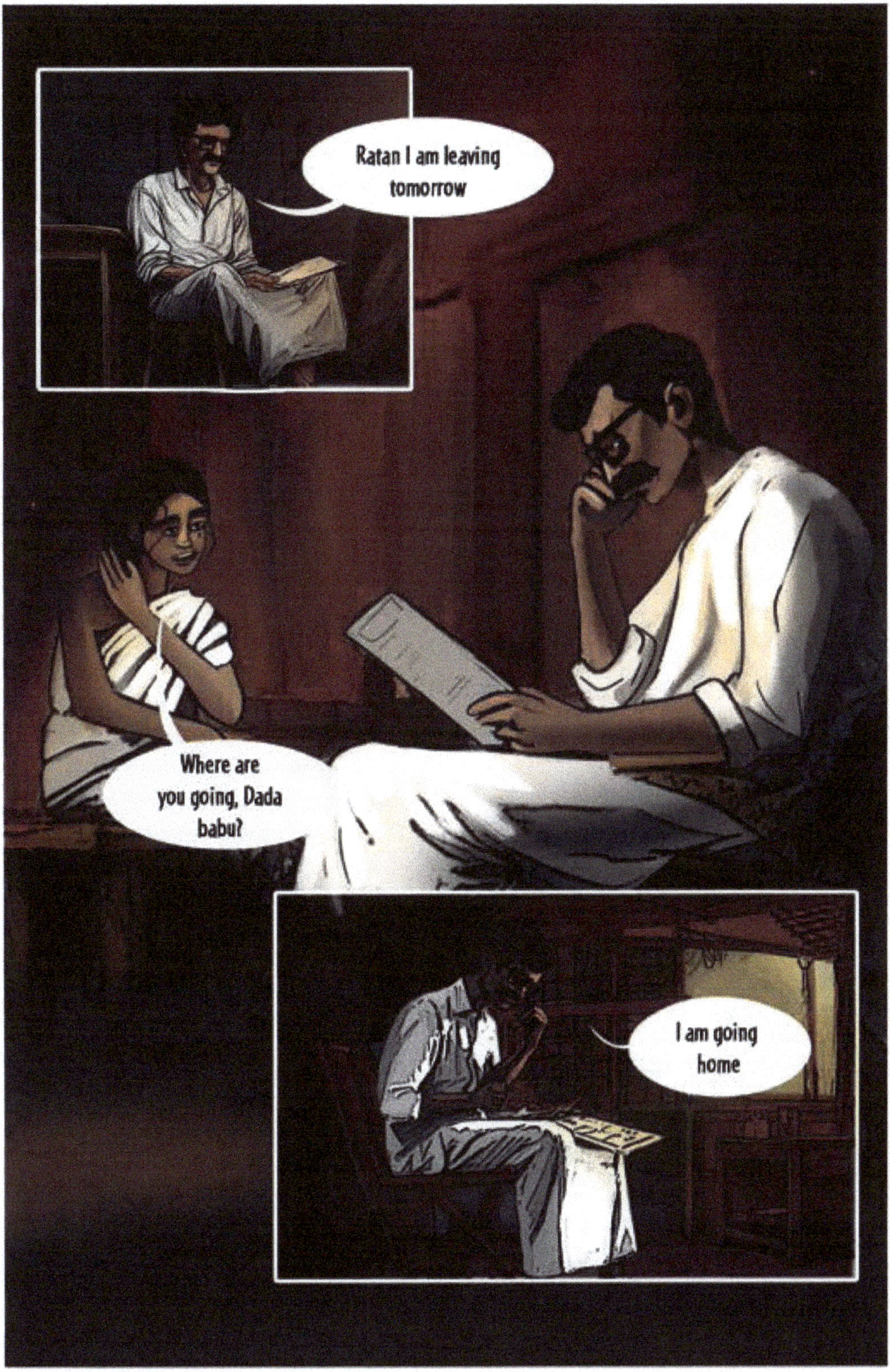
Ratan I am leaving tomorrow
Where are you going, Dada babu?
I am going home

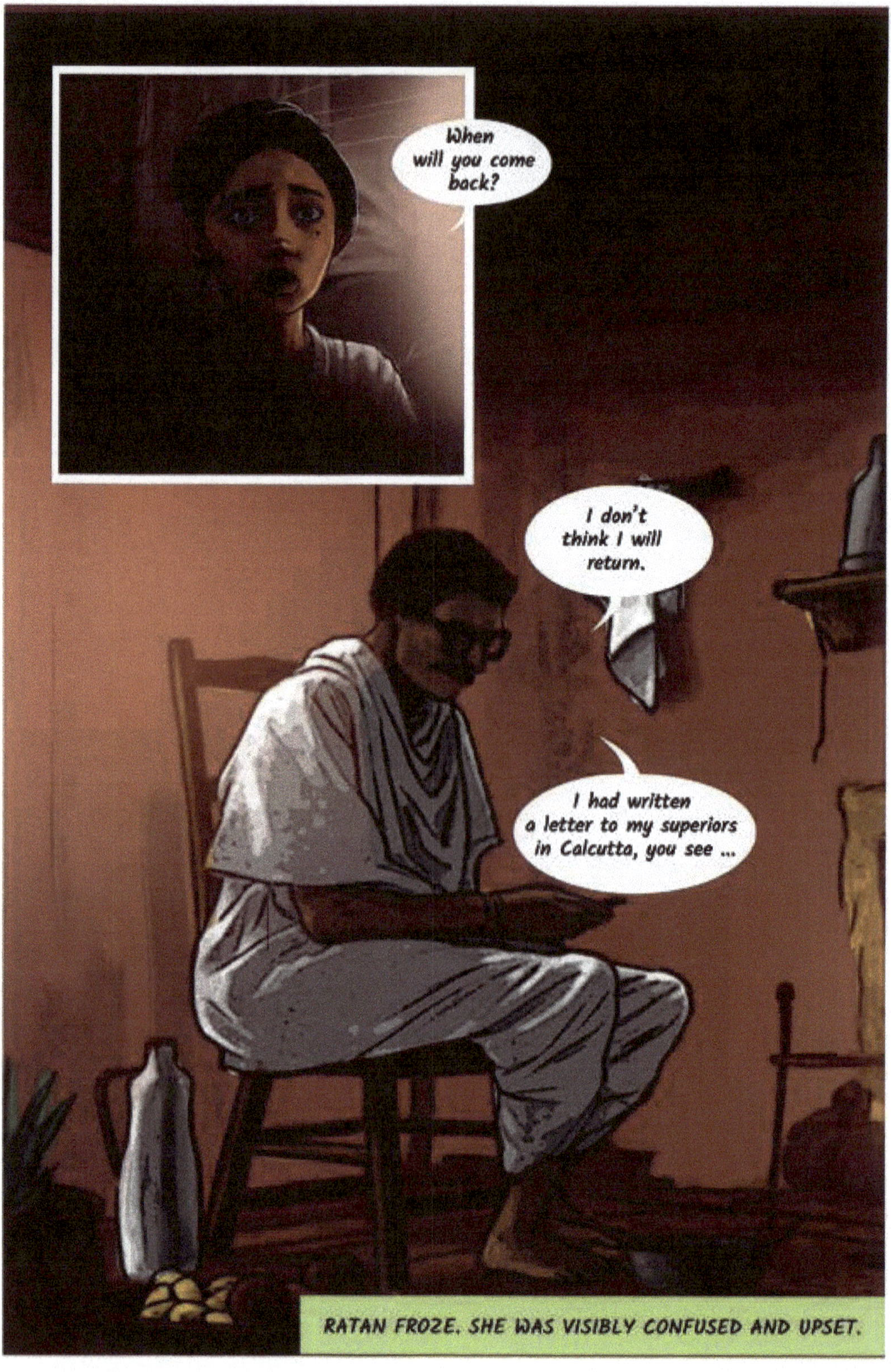
When will you come back?
I don't think I will return.
I had written a letter to my superiors in Calcutta, you see ...
RATAN FROZE. SHE WAS VISIBLY CONFUSED AND UPSET.

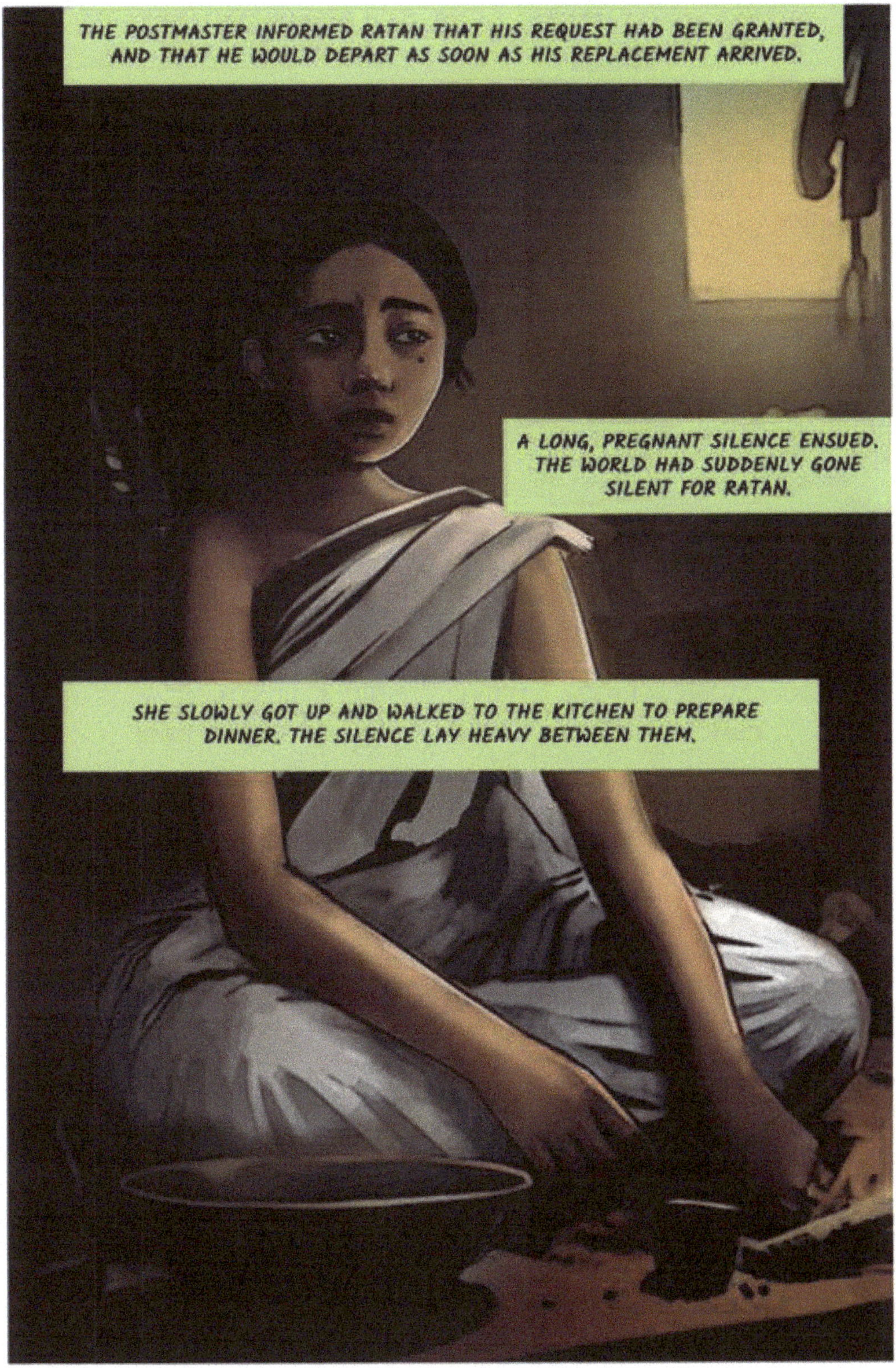
THE POSTMASTER INFORMED RATAN THAT HIS REQUEST HAD BEEN GRANTED, AND THAT HE WOULD DEPART AS SOON AS HIS REPLACEMENT ARRIVED.
A LONG, PREGNANT SILENCE ENSUED. THE WORLD HAD SUDDENLY GONE SILENT FOR RATAN.
SHE SLOWLY GOT UP AND WALKED TO THE KITCHEN TO PREPARE DINNER. THE SILENCE LAY HEAVY BETWEEN THEM.

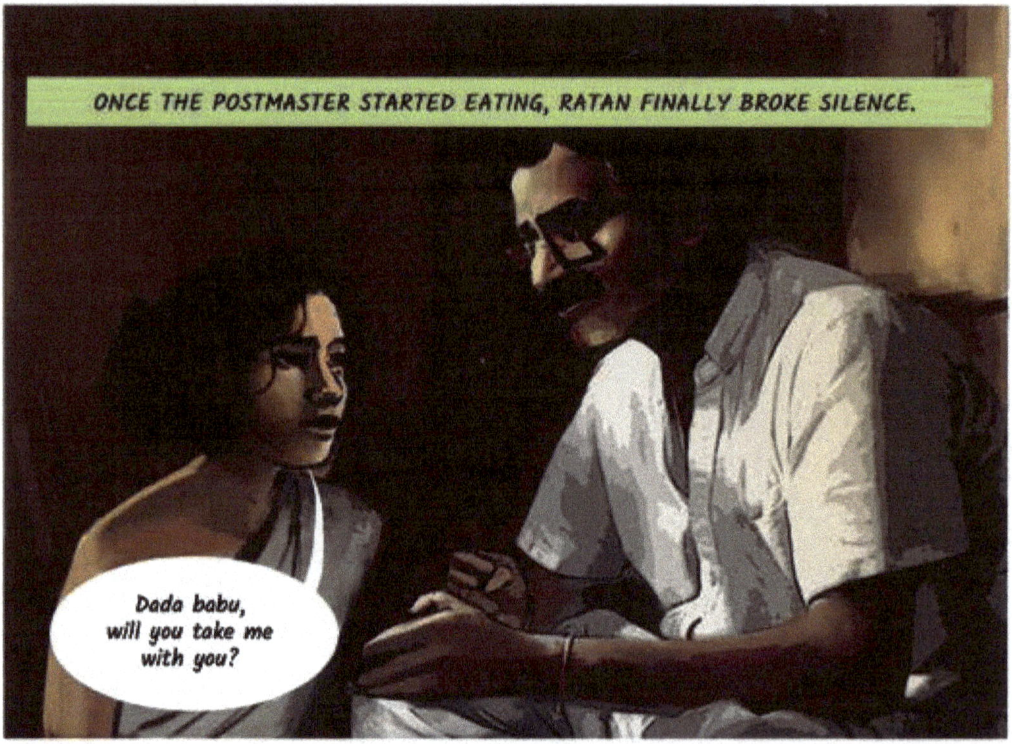
ONCE THE POSTMASTER STARTED EATING, RATAN FINALLY BROKE SILENCE.
Dada babu, will you take me with you?

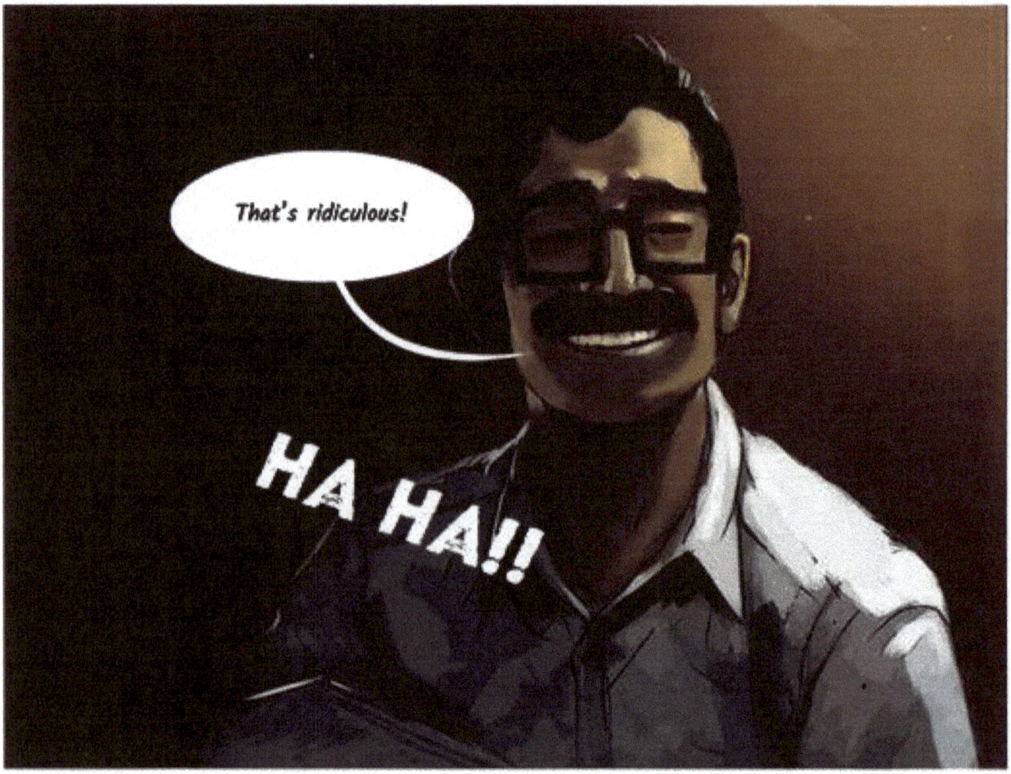
That's ridiculous!
HA HA!!

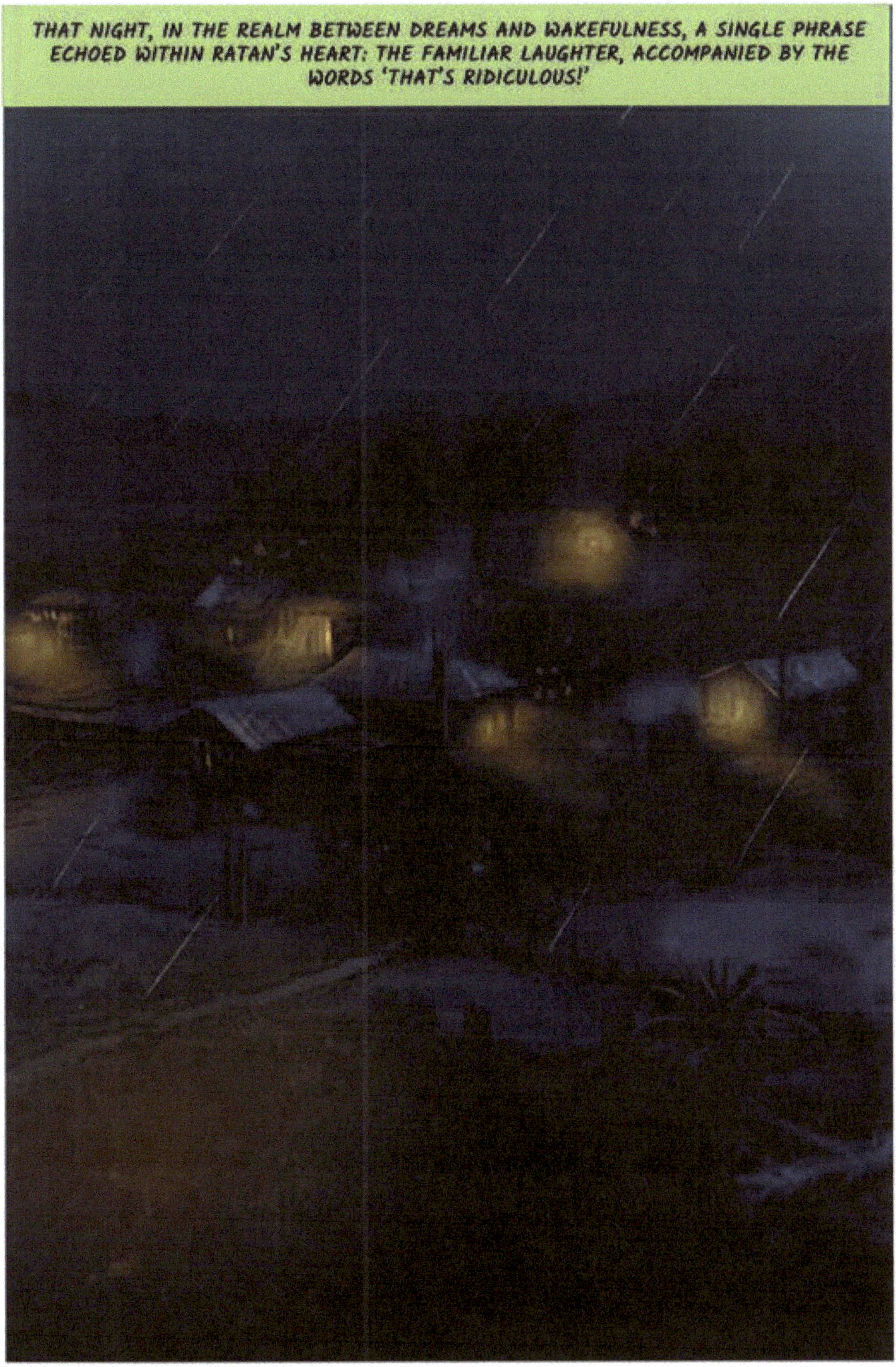
THAT NIGHT, IN THE REALM BETWEEN DREAMS AND WAKEFULNESS, A SINGLE PHRASE ECHOED WITHIN RATAN'S HEART: THE FAMILIAR LAUGHTER, ACCOMPANIED BY THE WORDS 'THAT'S RIDICULOUS!'

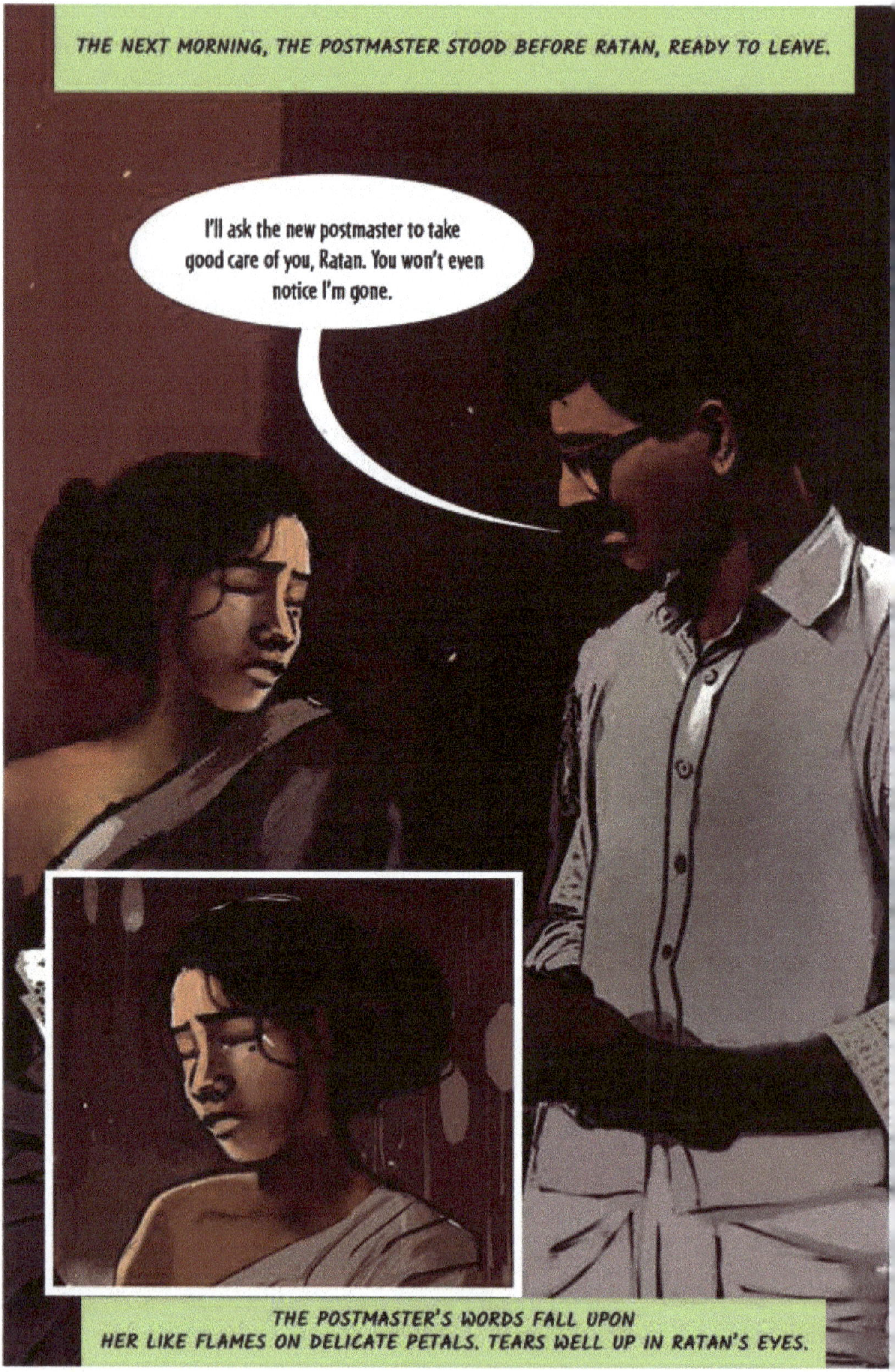
THE NEXT MORNING, THE POSTMASTER STOOD BEFORE RATAN, READY TO LEAVE.
I'll ask the new postmaster to take good care of you, Ratan. You won't even notice I'm gone.
THE POSTMASTER'S WORDS FALL UPON HER LIKE FLAMES ON DELICATE PETALS. TEARS WELL UP IN RATAN'S EYES.

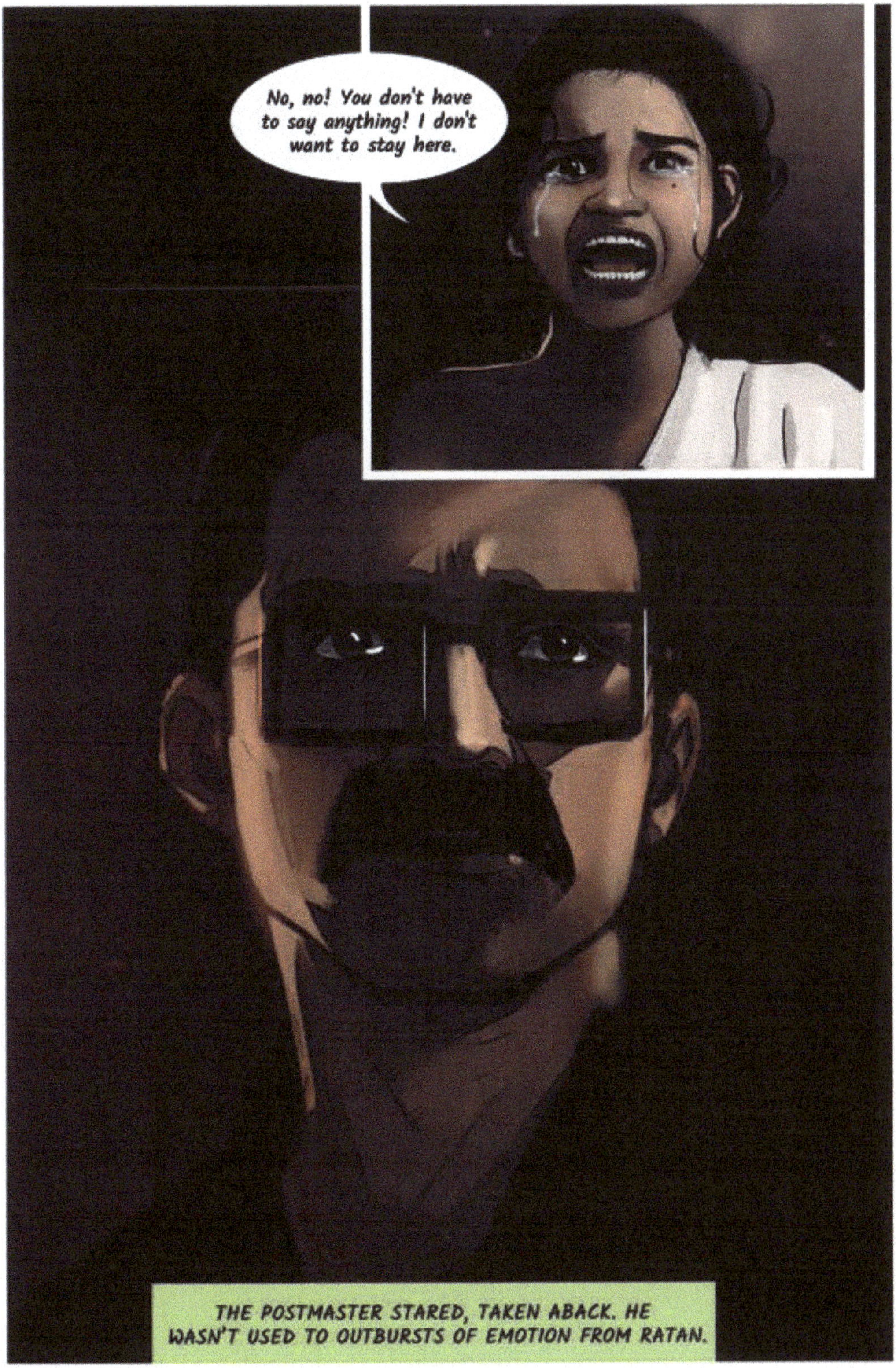
No, no! You don't have to say anything! I don't want to stay here.
THE POSTMASTER STARED, TAKEN ABACK. HE WASN'T USED TO OUTBURSTS OF EMOTION FROM RATAN.

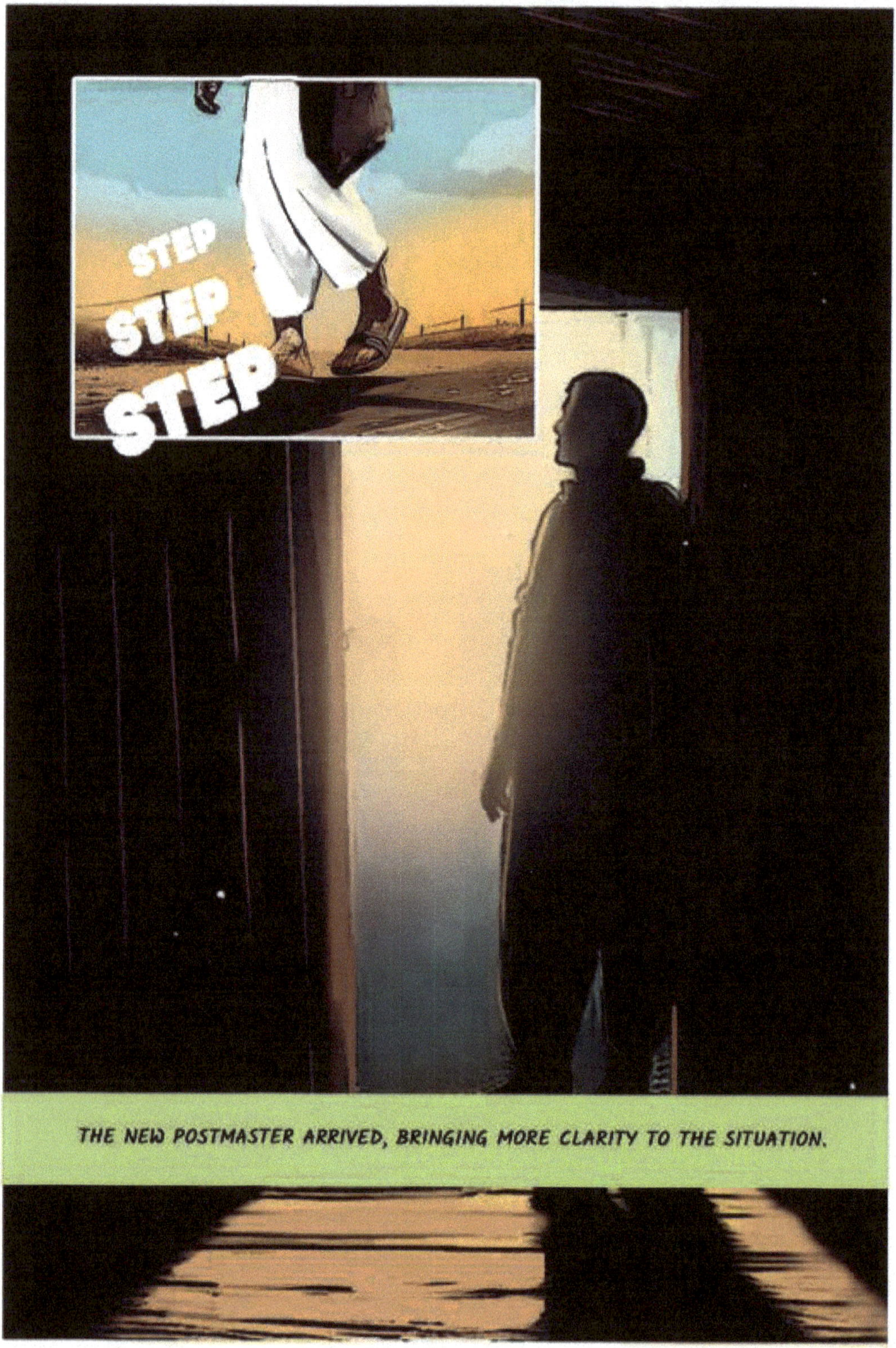
STEP
STEP
STEP
THE NEW POSTMASTER ARRIVED, BRINGING MORE CLARITY TO THE SITUATION.

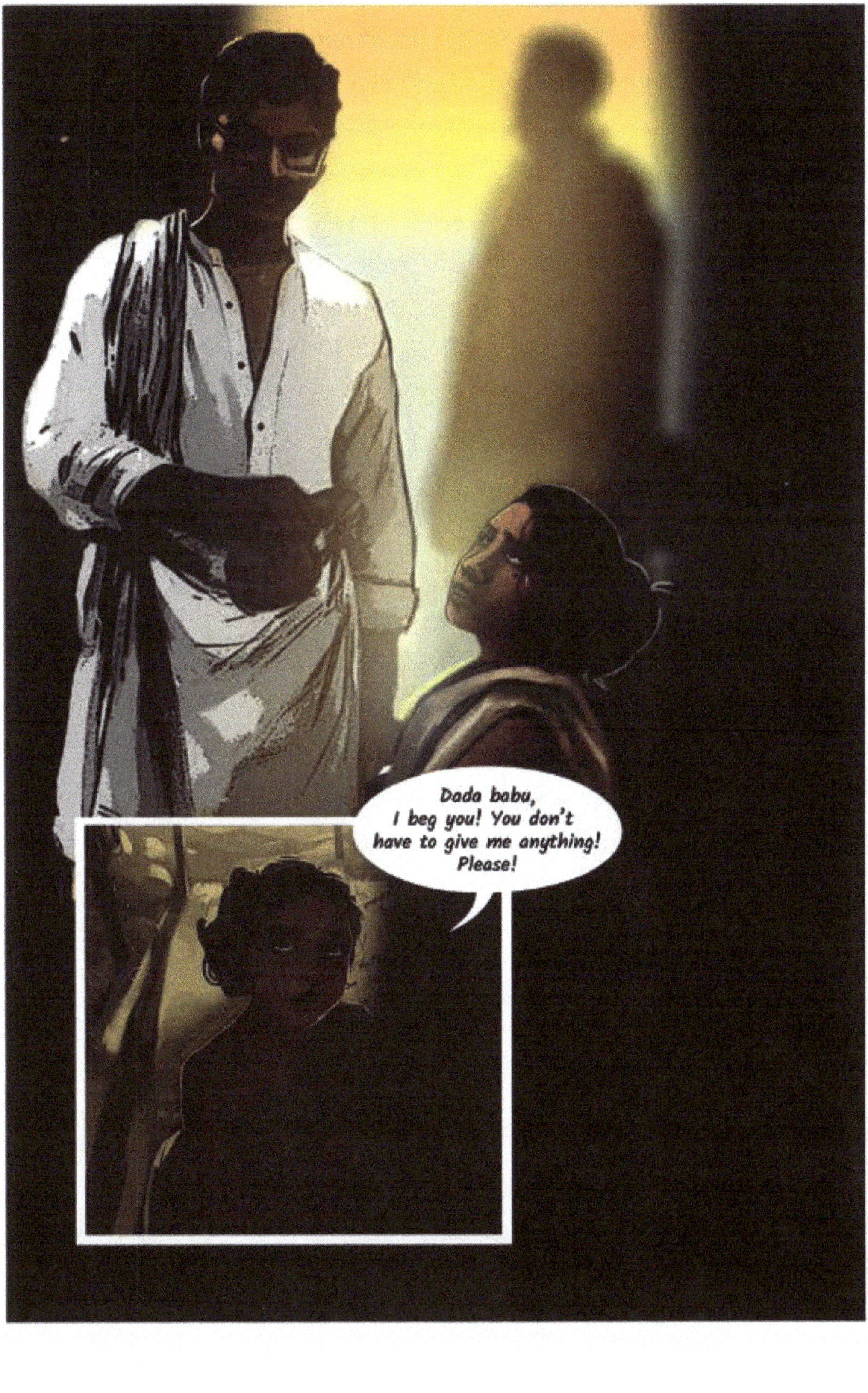
Dada babu, I beg you! You don't have to give me anything! Please!

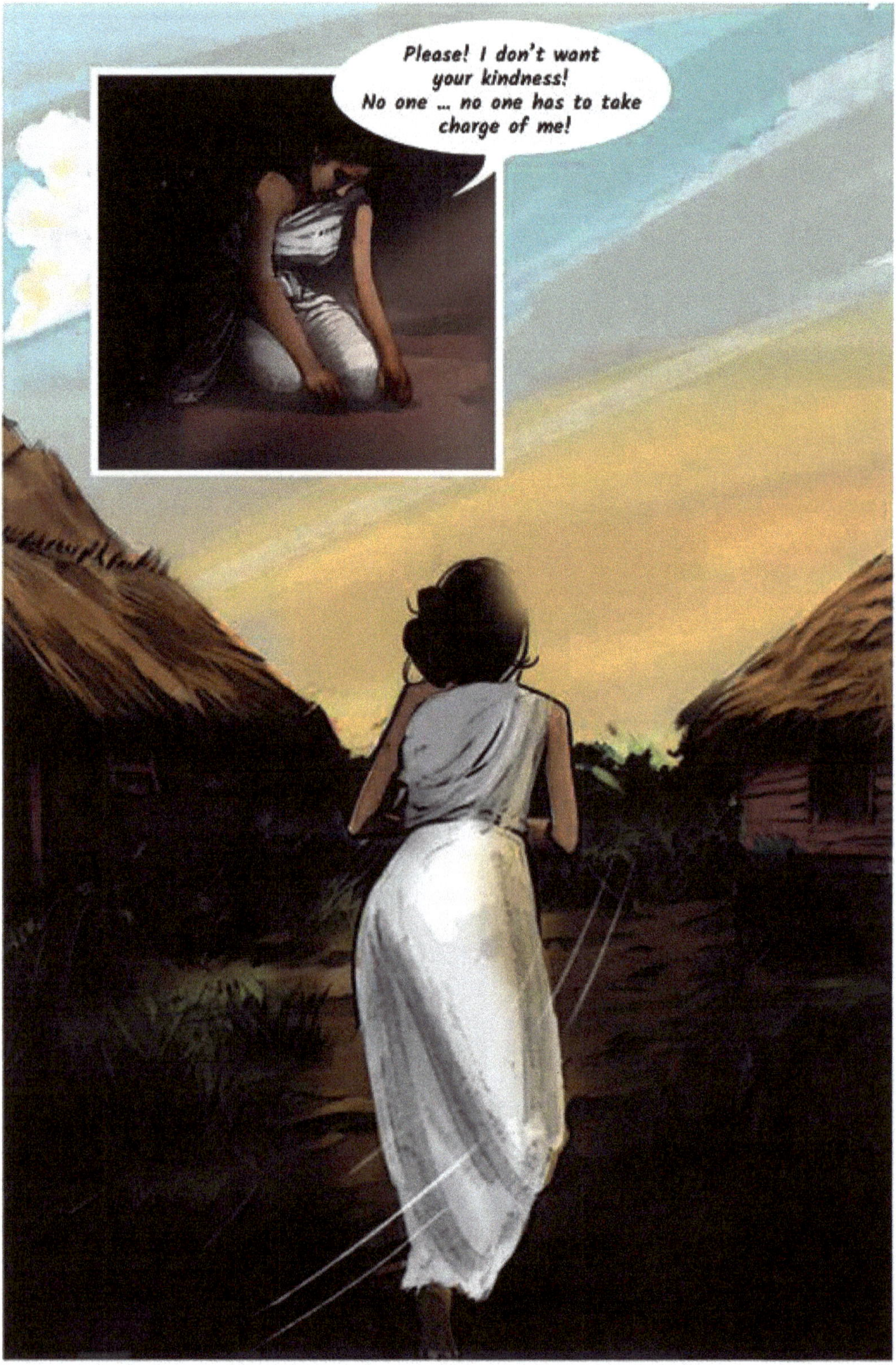
Please! I don't want your kindness! No one ... no one has to take charge of me!

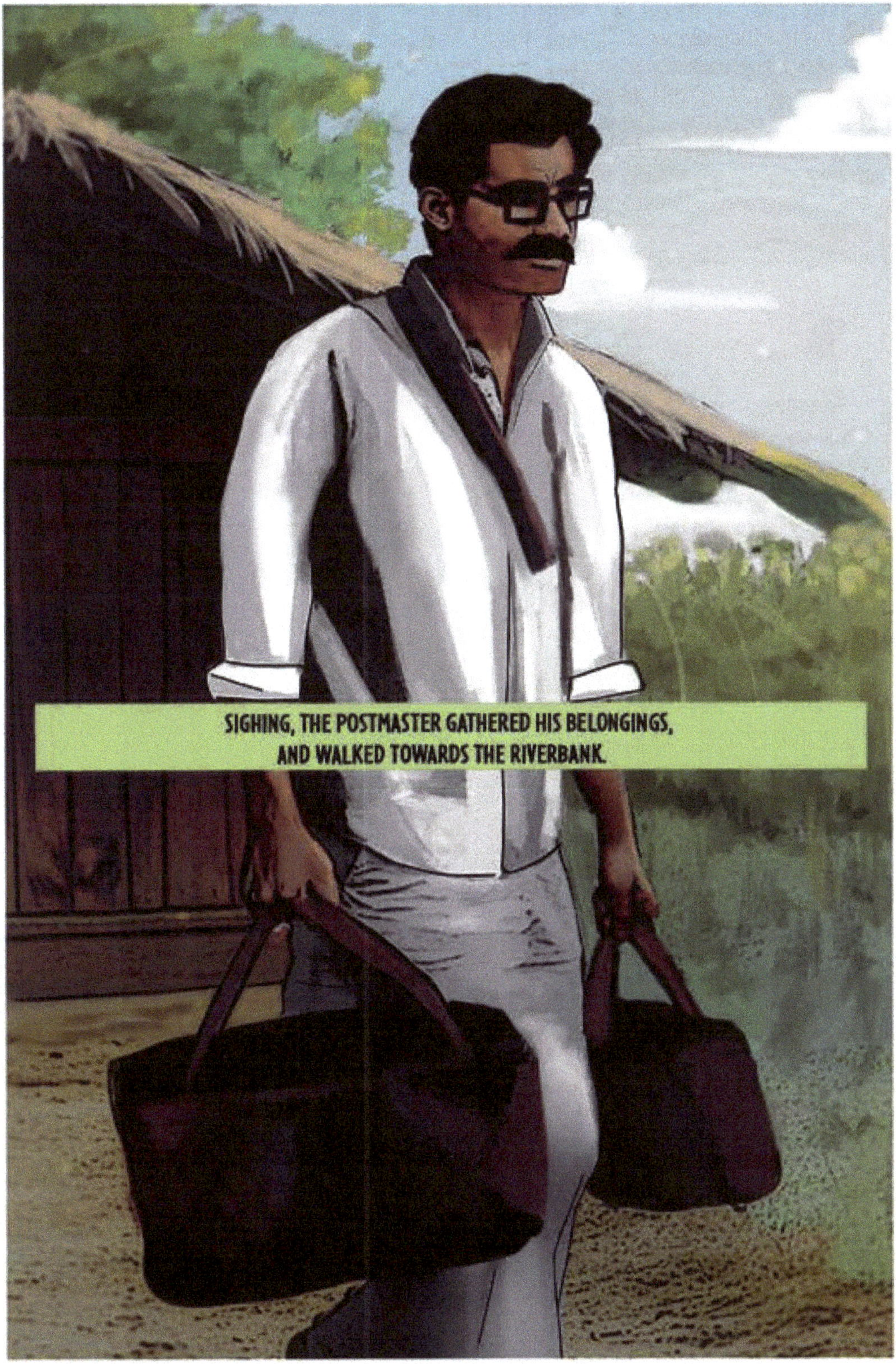
SIGHING, THE POSTMASTER GATHERED HIS BELONGINGS,
AND WALKED TOWARDS THE RIVERBANK.

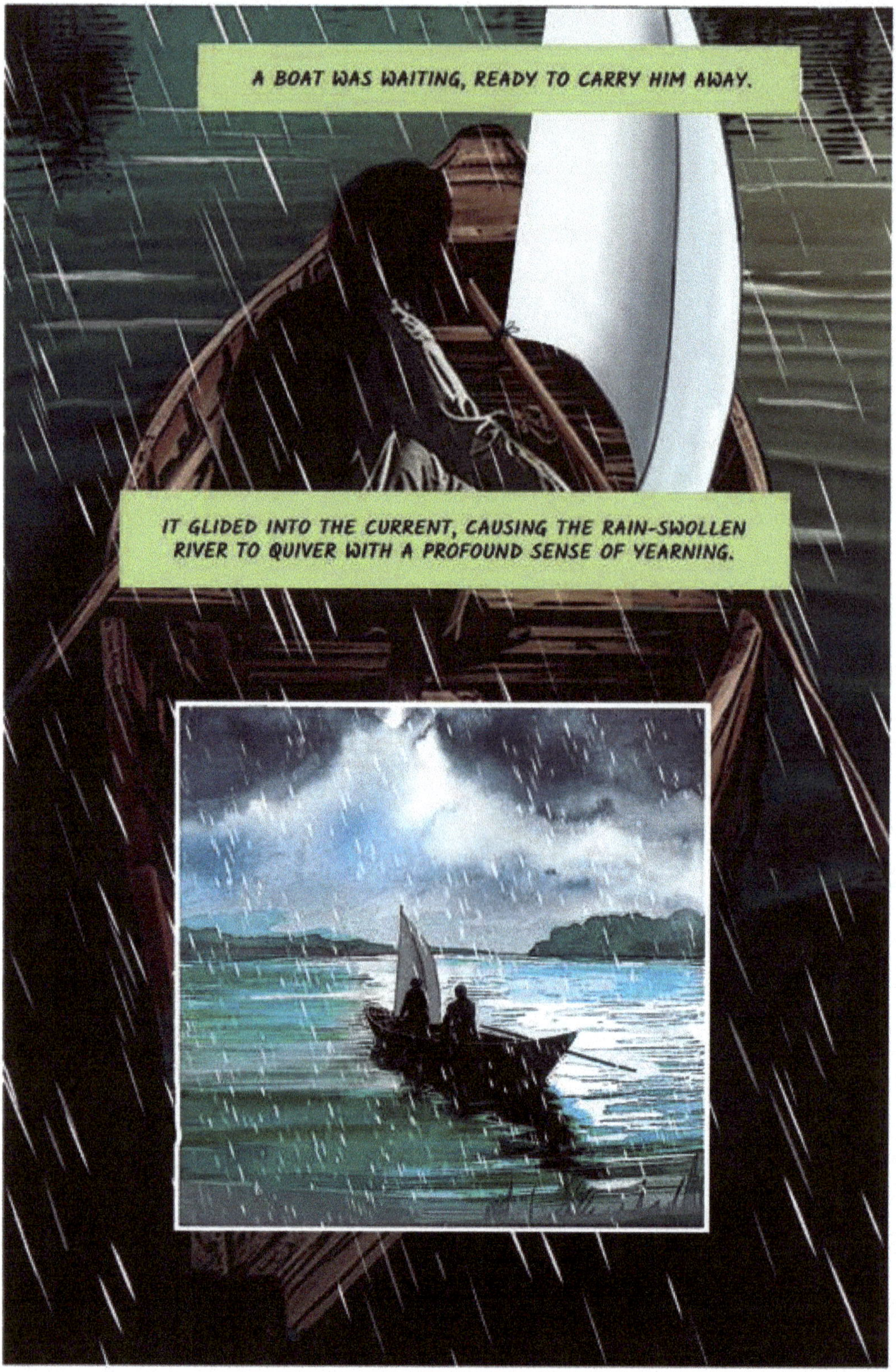
A BOAT WAS WAITING, READY TO CARRY HIM AWAY.
IT GLIDED INTO THE CURRENT, CAUSING THE RAIN-SWOLLEN RIVER TO QUIVER WITH A PROFOUND SENSE OF YEARNING.

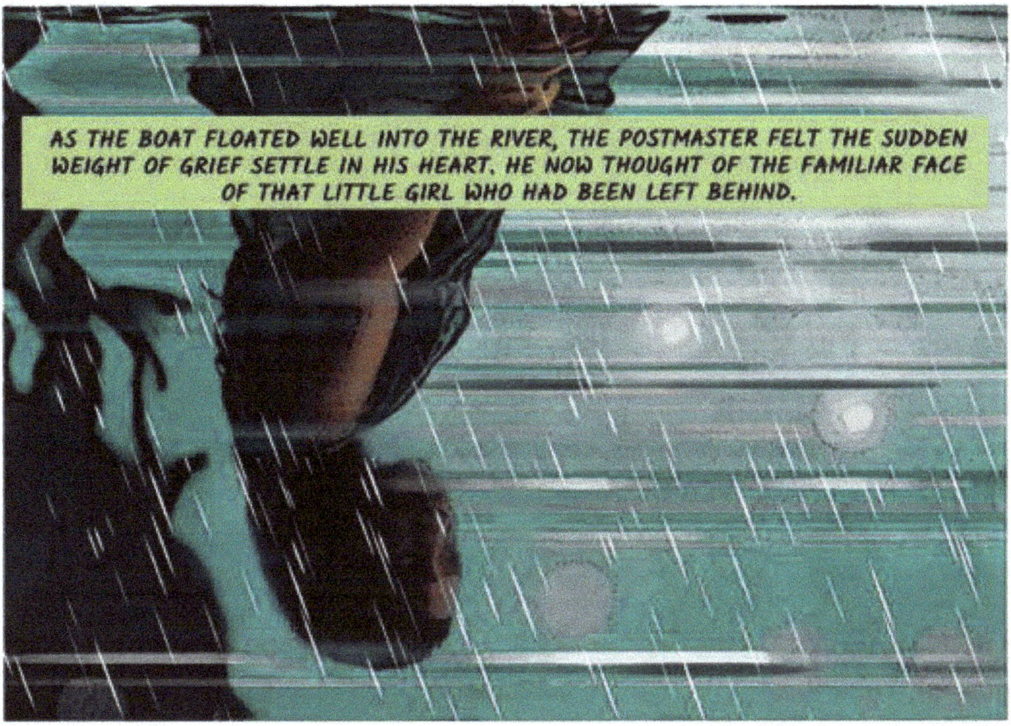
AS THE BOAT FLOATED WELL INTO THE RIVER, THE POSTMASTER FELT THE SUDDEN WEIGHT OF GRIEF SETTLE IN HIS HEART. HE NOW THOUGHT OF THE FAMILIAR FACE OF THAT LITTLE GIRL WHO HAD BEEN LEFT BEHIND.

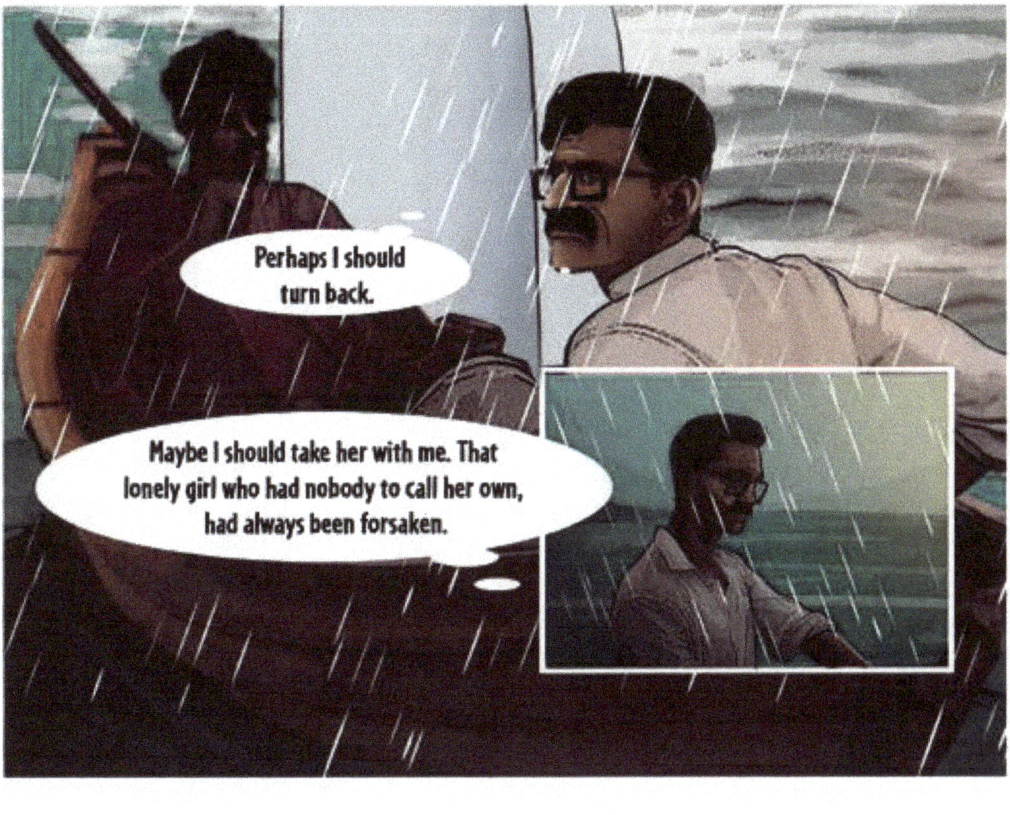
Perhaps I should turn back.
Maybe I should take her with me. That lonely girl who had nobody to call her own, had always been forsaken.

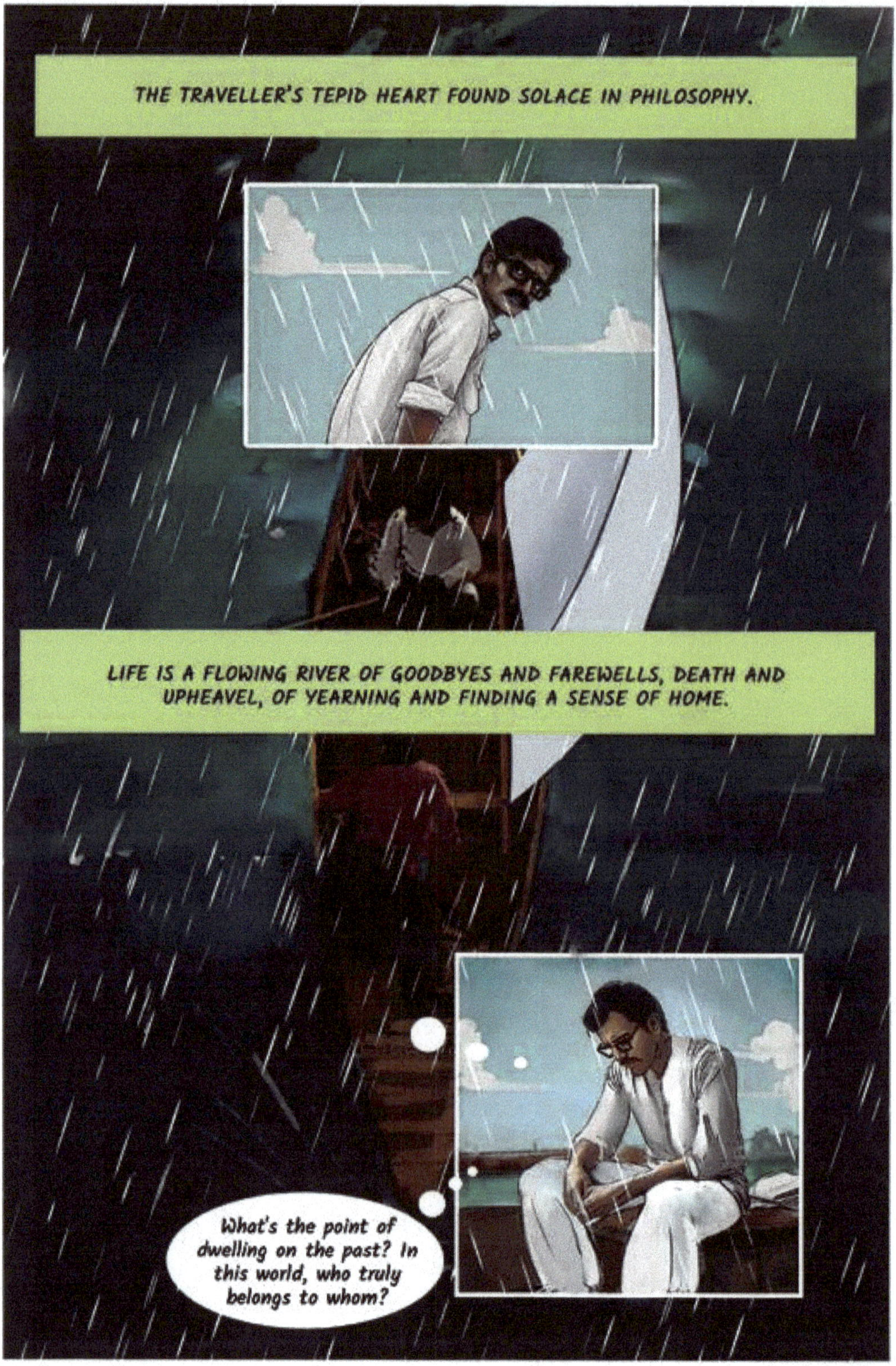
THE TRAVELLER'S TEPID HEART FOUND SOLACE IN PHILOSOPHY.
LIFE IS A FLOWING RIVER OF GOODBYES AND FAREWELLS, DEATH AND UPHEAVEL, OF YEARNING AND FINDING A SENSE OF HOME.
What's the point of dwelling on the past? In this world, who truly belongs to whom?

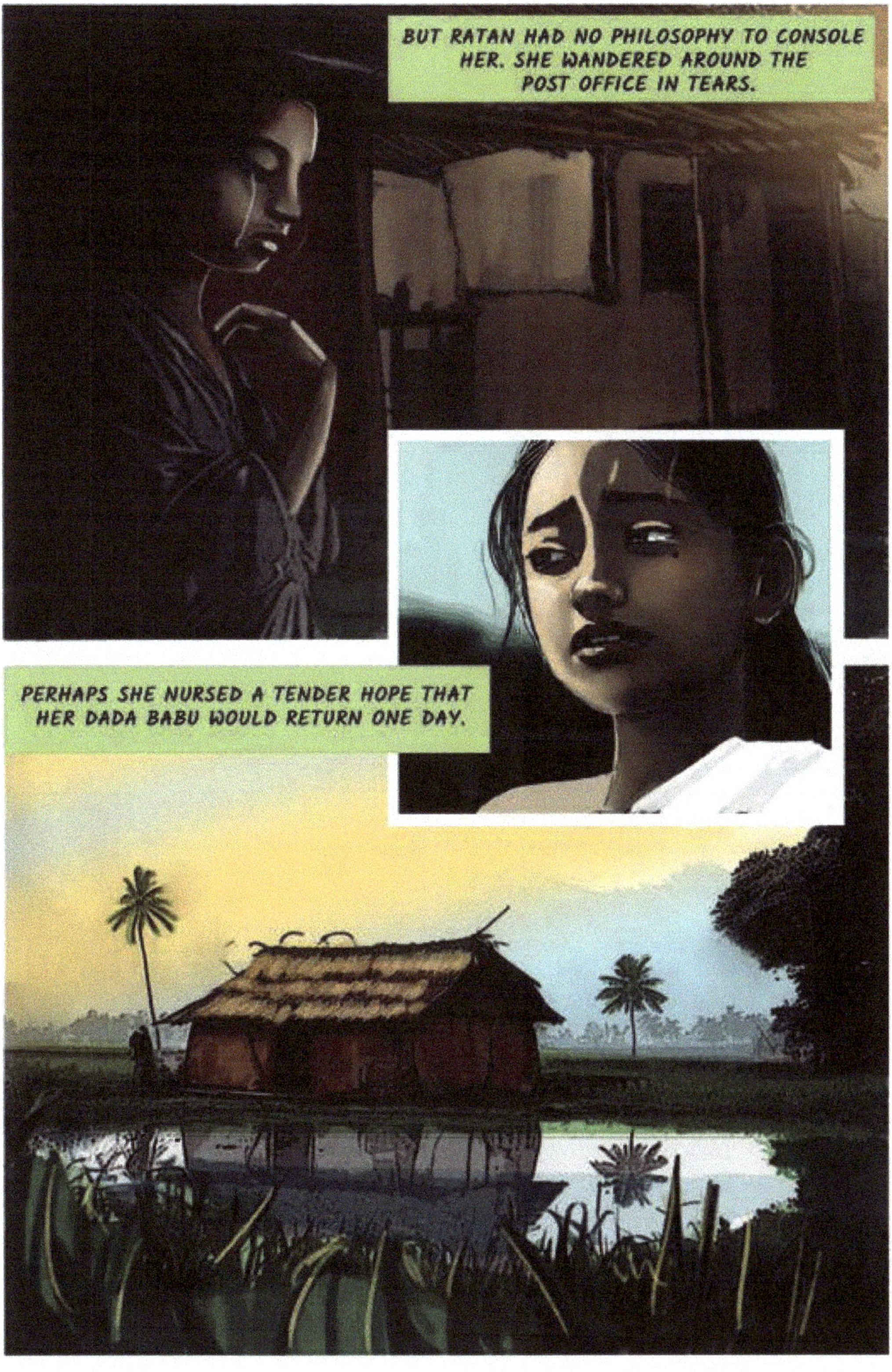
BUT RATAN HAD NO PHILOSOPHY TO CONSOLE HER. SHE WANDERED AROUND THE POST OFFICE IN TEARS.
PERHAPS SHE NURSED A TENDER HOPE THAT HER DADA BABU WOULD RETURN ONE DAY.

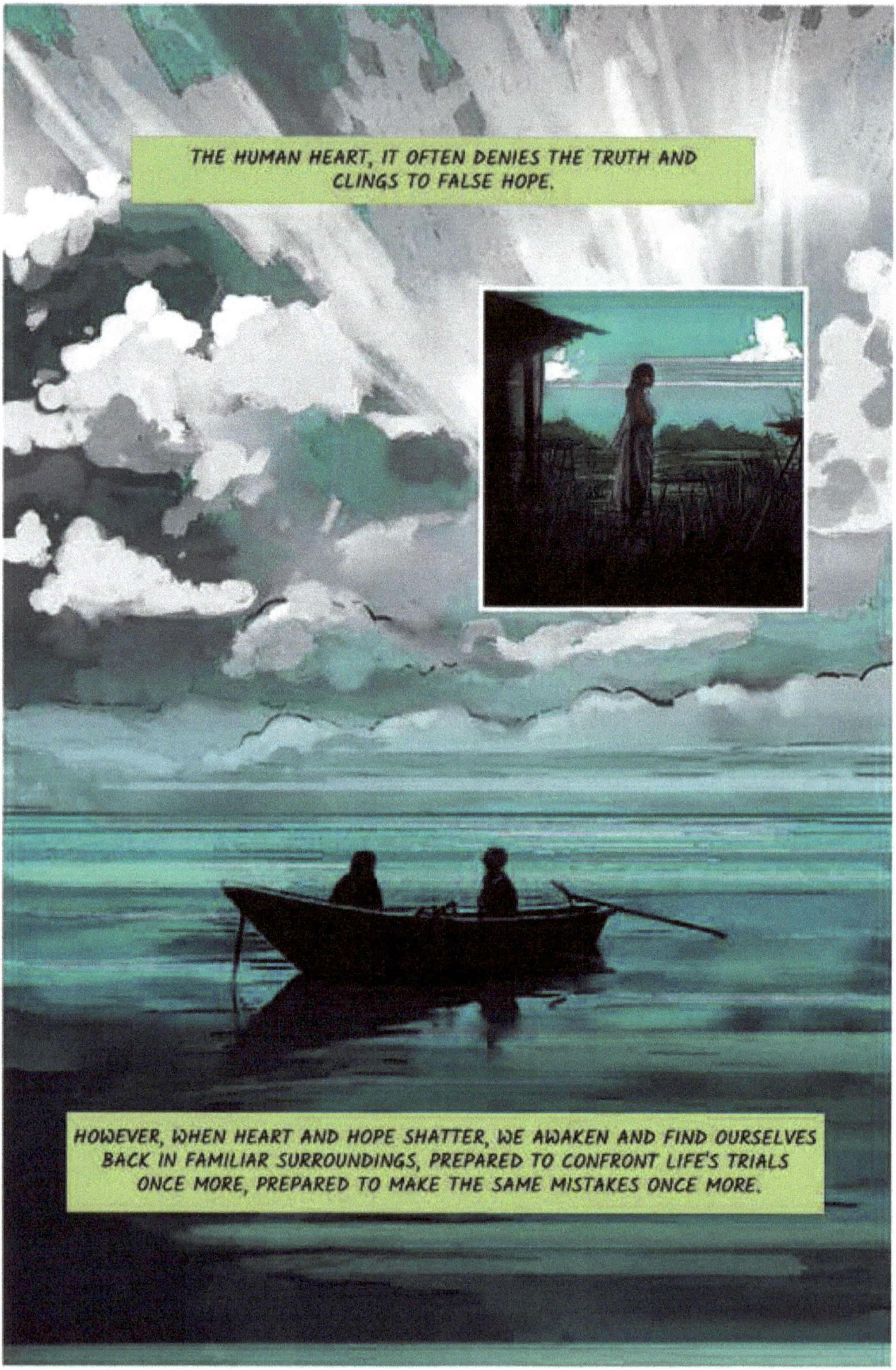
THE HUMAN HEART, IT OFTEN DENIES THE TRUTH AND CLINGS TO FALSE HOPE.
HOWEVER, WHEN HEART AND HOPE SHATTER, WE AWAKEN AND FIND OURSELVES BACK IN FAMILIAR SURROUNDINGS, PREPARED TO CONFRONT LIFE'S TRIALS ONCE MORE, PREPARED TO MAKE THE SAME MISTAKES ONCE MORE.

www.ingramcontent.com/pod-product-compliance
Lightning Source LLC
LaVergne TN
LVHW061626070526
838199LV00070B/6593